C000061574

A Primer on Efficiency Measurement for Utilities and Transport Regulators

Tim Coelli
Antonio Estache
Sergio Perelman
Lourdes Trujillo

This primer is supplemented by a database and computer software
that allows the reader to practice the example described in chapter 4.
Visit: http://www.worldbank.org/wbi/regulation/pubs/efficiencybook.html.

The World Bank
Washington, D.C.

The World Bank Institute was established by the World Bank in 1955 to train officials concerned with development planning, policymaking, investment analysis, and project implementation in member developing countries. At present the substance of WBI's work emphasizes macroeconomic and sectoral policy analysis. Through a variety of courses, seminars, workshops, and other learning activities, most of which are given overseas in cooperation with local institutions, WBI seeks to sharpen analytical skills used in policy analysis and to broaden understanding of the experience of individual countries with economic and social development. Although WBI's publications are designed to support its training activities, many are of interest to a much broader audience.

This report has been prepared by the staff of the World Bank. The judgments expressed do not necessarily reflect the views of the Board of Executive Directors or of the governments they represent.

The material in this publication is copyrighted. The World Bank encourages dissemination of its work and will normally grant permission promptly.

Permission to photocopy items for internal or personal use, for the internal or personal use of specific clients, or for educational classroom use is granted by the World Bank, provided that the appropriate fee is paid directly to the Copyright Clearance Center, Inc., 222 Rosewood Drive, Danvers, MA 01923, U.S.A., telephone 978-750-8400, fax 978-750-4470. Please contact the Copyright Clearance Center before photocopying items.

For permission to reprint individual articles or chapters, please fax your request with complete information to the Republication Department, Copyright Clearance Center, fax 978-750-4470.

All other queries on rights and licenses should be addressed to the World Bank at the address above or faxed to 202-522-2422.

The backlist of publications by the World Bank is shown in the annual *Index of Publications*, which is available from the Office of the Publisher.

ISBN 0-8213-5379-9

Library of Congress Cataloging-in-Publication Data has been applied for.

Contents

Foreword

The infrastructure privatization wave of the 1990s changed, but did not eliminate, the government's role in the sector. The scope for introducing competition continues to be limited in many parts of infrastructure businesses, resulting in private monopolies operating at least some segments of most utilities and transport services. Among the main responsibilities of infrastructure regulators are the design and implementation of regulatory processes that will ensure the fair distribution of the gains from the transfer of services to private monopolies. This mandate means that regulators must be able to assess the extent to which the regulated operators are managing to improve efficiency after taking over from public operators. For many of the new regulators implementing this mandate has been tougher than expected. Even more difficult is their role in expanding services to the unserved.

This book, the fourth in a recent series of World Bank Institute books on infrastructure regulation, is intended to help regulators learn about the tools needed to measure efficiency. It is based on lecture notes from courses the World Bank Institute offers in English, French, and Spanish throughout the developing world and has benefited from feedback received during those courses. It provides an overview of the various dimensions of efficiency that regulators should be concerned with. It also summarizes the main quantification techniques available to facilitate decisions in the most common regulatory processes. The issues covered should be of particular interest to those policymakers and regulators interested in measuring relative efficiency and in implementing any incentive-based regulatory mechanism that requires the measurement of efficiency, such as price caps, revenue caps, or yardstick competition. The book focuses on methodology selection, data collection, and related issues.

This is not an easy topic, but the book does provide readers with all the conceptual tools they need to make real-life decisions. It is also supported by a web site from which readers can download software they can use to implement the techniques described. The web site also includes a database that will allow readers to try to reproduce the empirical example provided in chapter 4.

I hope that this *Primer on Efficiency Measurement* will be as useful to infrastructure regulators and policymakers as the previous books have been and that it will help enhance the quality and transparency of dialogue among the actors involved in infrastructure provision and reform.

Frannie A. Léautier
Vice President
World Bank Institute

About the Authors

Tim Coelli is a professor of economics at the University of Queensland, Australia. He specializes in theoretical and applied econometrics, production economics, and performance measurement. He has worked as a consultant for the Independent Pricing and Regulatory Tribunal of New South Wales, the Water Services Association of Australia, and the Queensland Water Reform Unit. Email: t.coelli@economics.uq.edu.au.

Antonio Estache is an economic advisor at the World Bank and a research fellow at the European Center for Advanced Research in Economics and Statistics, Université Libre de Bruxelles. He specializes in industrial organization and regulatory economics. He has advised many governments in Africa, Asia, and Latin America on infrastructure sector reform and regulation. Email: aestache@worldbank.org.

Sergio Perelman is a professor of economics at the University of Liège, where he is also director of the Center of Research in Public and Population Economics. He specializes in applied econometrics and performance measurement and has been working on policy-oriented research projects across Europe. Email: sergio.perelman@ulg.ac.be.

Lourdes Trujillo is the director of the Department of Applied Economic Analysis of the University of Las Palmas of Grand Canary. She is a professor of microeconomics and specializes in the empirical analysis of network industries. She has advised many governments in Latin America on transport sector reform and regulation. Email: lourdes@empresariales.ulpgc.es.

Acknowledgments

In writing this book we have benefited from discussions with Ian Alexander, Antonio Alvarez, Phil Burns, Javier Campos, José Carbajo, Luis Correia, Claude Crampes, Alex Galetovic, Andres Gomez-Lobo, Phil Gray, Shawna Grosskopf, Alan Horncastle, Marc Ivaldi, Racine Kane, Eugene Kouassi, Gustavo Nombela, Paul Noumba, Martin Rodriguez-Pardina, Martin Rossi, Christian Ruzzier, and many regulators in Latin America and Africa who have participated in World Bank–sponsored training. Furthermore, we would like to express our thanks to Knox Lovell, who provided extensive comments on an earlier draft of this book. Finally, any mistakes and all interpretations of facts are ours and do not engage in any way the institutions we are affiliated with.

Abbreviations and Acronyms

AE	Allocative efficiency
AEC	Allocative efficiency change
CAPM	Capital asset pricing model
CE	Cost efficiency
CEC	Cost efficiency change
CPI	Consumer price index
CRB	Coelli, Rao, and Battese (1998)
CRS	Constant returns to scale
DEA	Data envelopment analysis
DEAP	Data envelopment analysis program
kl	Kiloliter
km	Kilometer
kWh	Kilowatt hour
LLF	Log-likelihood function
OLS	Ordinary least squares
PIN	Price-based index number

SE	Scale efficiency
SEC	Scale efficiency change
SFA	Stochastic frontier analysis
TC	Technical change
TE	Technical efficiency
TEC	Technical efficiency change
TFP	Total factor productivity
TFPC	Total factor productivity change
VRS	Variable returns to scale
WACC	Weighted average cost of capital

1

Introduction

Until relatively recently infrastructure services—electricity, gas, water, sewerage, telecommunications, airports, ports, and rail transport—were provided by vertically and horizontally integrated public firms that also tended to be self-regulated (the United States, where many infrastructure firms have been privately owned and regulated for some time, is an exception). The infrastructure privatization waves of the 1990s that spread across developing countries and some countries of the Organisation for Economic Co-operation and Development, most notably Australia, New Zealand, and the United Kingdom and a few other European countries, have changed the institutional structure of this sector as well as the policy agenda. The desire to create a competitive environment is now prevailing in infrastructure industries, and where competition is limited the search for efficiency gains is at the core of the regulation debate.

Countries have generally assigned the responsibility for regulation to new, relatively autonomous agencies, which are now learning to cope with their mandates. Evidence from the last decade suggests that in both industrial and developing countries, these mandates are proving to be tougher than expected for many of the new regulators. Information asymmetries between monitoring agencies and monitored firms are the norm rather than the exception, in particular, on the cost side of the business. This reduces monitoring agencies' ability to carry out their role of watchdog of operators. It also reduces their ability to ensure that the efficiency gains from potential or effective competition are shared fairly between operators and users. This inability to organize a fair sharing of the efficiency gains, which does not hurt firms' incentives to perform well, is a major source of criticism of the performance of the new regulators and a source of conflict between operators and users.[1] It also explains the increased interest among monitoring agencies, producers, and users alike in the quantitative measurement of these gains.[2]

This book is written as a manual to support a series of courses put together by the World Bank Institute, but also to help regulators go through the relevant academic literature, which has become quite technical and often assumes a level of knowledge that most policymakers and regulators do not have. For interested regulators the book also provides practical advice on how to conduct an empirical analysis of efficiency in the infrastructure industries. The necessary software and examples are available on the World Bank Institute web site (http://www.worldbank.org/wbi/regulation/pubs/efficiencybook.html). The methods discussed here are equally applicable to situations where the firms are publicly owned, privately owned, or some combination of the two. The issues covered should be of particular interest to those regulatory authorities that are required to obtain measures of relative efficiency and of historical productivity growth and to assist with the setting of price caps or of any incentive-based regulatory mechanism requiring the measurement of efficiency, such as yardstick competition. The focus is on methodology selection, data collection, and related issues.

The book is designed to be self-contained for regulators that need to focus on measuring the efficiency of the firms they are monitoring. While some sections of the book may appear to be somewhat technical and overwhelming to some readers, it is designed to allow interested users to actually undertake studies relevant to their sector. All the relevant steps are discussed, explained, and eventually illustrated. Earlier drafts of the book have been tested by various analysts new to the topic and have benefited from their suggestions to ensure that it is as complete as possible in regard to the practice of efficiency measurement for regulated industries.

---

1. The price cap revisions in the electricity and gas sectors in Argentina are good illustrations of the type of conflict that can arise (see, for example, Estache and Rodriguez-Pardina 2000).

2. The Australian, Dutch, and U.K. regulators have been among the most rigorous participants in this debate and their various web sites are useful sources of information. See, for example, http://www.accc.gov.au, http://www.ipart. nsw.gov.au, http://www.reggen.vic.gov.au, http://www.dte.nl, http:// www.open.gov.uk/ofwat, and http://www.open.gov.uk/ofgen. For a more traditional approach to benchmarking in the water sector see http://www. worldbank.org/html/fpd/water/topics/uom_bench.html.

The book avoids detailed discussions of economic theory and econometric methodology, as these are available elsewhere. Readers may refer to Laffont and Tirole (1993) for a comprehensive treatment of the economic theory of the regulated firm, Bogetoft (1994, 1995, 1997) and Agrell, Bogetoft, and Tind (2002) for an extension of the incentive regulation theory in a benchmark and yardstick competition scheme, and to Armstrong, Cowan, and Vickers (1994) or Newbery (2000) for an interpretation of the importance of these principles in practice. A particularly relevant reading is Bernstein and Sappington (1999), which provides a systematic overview of the criteria for picking an efficiency measure in the context of price regulation. Finally, while this book provides many insights into the various efficiency measurement methodologies, it does not claim to be a rigorous introduction to these methodologies. For the interested reader Coelli, Rao, and Battese (1998) (hereafter referred to as CRB) provide a much more rigorous overview of methods and conceptual issues.

2

Why Should Regulators
Be Interested in Efficiency?

Efficiency is at the core of many of the standard responsibilities assigned to regulators. The most common instance in which a government agency should be interested in measuring efficiency is when implementing some type of incentive-based regulation in a specific infrastructure sector. These types of regulatory regimes, such as price cap regulation, aim at promoting efficiency among operators. Regulators may also be interested in implementing comparative efficiency evaluations to promote yardstick competition. Indeed, in most cases regulators have multiple objectives, many of which have something to do with various aspects of efficiency.

To demonstrate that the concern for efficiency is quite real and pervasive among regulators, consider the case of the Argentinean land transport regulator, for instance, which is representative of many of the regulatory agencies created to monitor recent deregulation or privatization in developing economies. The decree that creates this regulatory agency and specifies its obligations suggests quite clearly that the promotion of efficiency in various forms is one of its main responsibilities.[1] This includes the obligation to ensure that

---

1. Government of Argentina Decree number 660 of June 24, 1996, in particular annex 1, where the regulator's responsibilities are defined as protecting the rights of users; promoting competition in the markets for transport services; ensuring better safety, operation, reliability, and equity; ensuring generalized use of the road transport and rail transport systems for passengers and freight; and ensuring appropriate progress in all modes (see Campos-Mendez, Estache, and Trujillo 2001).

- The interests of current users are taken into account in the operator's production decisions. In practice this means that the regulator should check that the operators minimize the cost of delivering their services while meeting all their contractual obligations. In more technical terms it means that the regulator must monitor the operator's cost efficiency.
- The sector is competitive, intermodal competition works, and all users are treated fairly. In a less positive way the regulator must check that users are not charged too much, that required subsidy levels are what the operators claim, and that hidden cross-subsidies are not relied on for anticompetitive or predatory behavior. In practice this means that the regulator must check that the price charged for every noncompetitive activity reflects its costs, assuming that every activity can be ring-fenced.[2] In more technical terms it means that the regulator must monitor output mix allocative efficiency.
- The sector grows appropriately, that is, that operators make the right investment, technology, and management choices to ensure that future demand will be met in a smooth way and that service rationing does not occur, all of which is also known as dynamic efficiency.

Implicitly, the decree states that for any period of observation, the regulator's performance assessments must offer a balanced view of the various sources of efficiency, which is a reasonable request on any regulatory agency, but assumes that the regulator is able to measure them. These obligations are representative of the challenges new regulators have to face in a difficult political context in most reforming countries. They need to monitor progress in the performance of the new operators of recently privatized public services to check if the improvements expected from a switch from public operators are real. This means that the performance improvements achieved through the reforms must, at least to some extent, be quantified if the gains are to be shared with users (or the losses shared with taxpayers) in a fair and transparent way.

The remainder of this chapter provides the various elements that justify why practitioners need this book.

---

2. By ring-fencing we refer to the organization of a firm's accounts so that the costs associated with various activities or outputs are clearly specified.

Regulation Methods

Most network industries, for example, utilities and transport, have natural monopoly characteristics. Economic theory indicates that if left unchecked, monopolies have the ability to exert their market power and set prices above costs so as to yield above normal profits. For much of the 20th century, the answer to this potential problem generally involved one of two options: (a) government ownership, or (b) private ownership combined with some form of cost-plus rate of return regulation, where the regulated firm is allowed to set prices so as to cover noncapital costs plus a fair rate of return on capital. The United States has favored the latter approach, while the United Kingdom and many other countries have favored the former approach (see Green and Rodriguez-Pardina 1999 for a longer discussion).

However, these two options are not without problems. In particular, both options suffer from a lack of efficiency incentives, which can result in costs that are above those that would exist in a competitive industry. This has led to the recent development of new forms of regulation that seek to be incentive compatible. U.K. telecommunications regulators championed these incentive regulation methods in the 1980s and many regulators in numerous industries around the world have since adopted them in various forms.

Incentive regulation can take various forms, but the most common form involves the application of some form of price cap regulation. Price cap regulation specifies the maximum rate at which regulated prices may change, after adjusting for inflation, over a specific time period, usually four or five years. In practice, these prices are usually set to increase at a rate equal to the rate of increase in the consumer price index (CPI) minus a so-called productivity offset, designated as X, and thus it is often called CPI-X regulation. The formula implies that consumers will face a nominal price decrease if inflation is lower than the X assessed for the period. The value of X is generally based on the regulator's assessment of the potential for productivity growth in the regulated firm. This is a crucial variable. If it is set too low, the firm is earning excessive profits because the tariff ends up being significantly higher than actual costs. If it is set too high, the firm may find itself in financial trouble because the tariff may no longer cover its real costs.

Estimating X is a complex matter. It is supposed to reflect the extent to which the regulated industry can improve its productivity faster than the rest of the economy in which it is operating, accounting for differences in the evolution of the input prices in the regulated industry compared with the input prices in the rest of the economy. Reasonable estimates of aggregate productivity gains are available in most countries, and this is not a major matter of concern here; however, in most countries regulators lack information at the sectoral level. Furthermore, in some cases the regulator may choose to set different X-factors for different firms in an industry if it has reason to believe that some firms are more inefficient relative to other firms.[3]

In practice, in preparation for tariff revision regulators will generally commission studies of previous total factor productivity (TFP) growth in the industry, and perhaps a study of the present levels of firm-level efficiency to help them set the X-factor for each firm in the industry. The X-factors are usually set so that firms are able to earn a fair rate of return on capital if they can achieve an efficient level of costs, as defined by the regulator. If the firm can contain cost increases below the allowed CPI-X price increase, they can pocket the difference, and hence earn above normal profits, that is, a higher rate of return on capital. This is the main incentive aspect of the method.

Practitioners of CPI-X regulation also stress that the performance measures used to set the X-factor for a firm must not be derived solely from the firm's past performance, because this will negate the incentives involved. That is, if a regulator assigns an X-factor of 3 percent per year to firm A because it achieved a TFP increase of 3 percent per year in recent years, firm A will have no incentive to attempt to increase its performance in the future, because it knows that it will lead to a larger X-factor in the next regulatory period. Thus the regulator must also use data from external benchmarks, such as other firms in the industry or international comparisons, to set the X-factors.

Thus to summarize, the selection of the X-factor is usually based on two pieces of information.

- What has the rate of productivity growth been in this industry in recent years?
- To what extent is this firm operating below best practice in this industry?

Without this information, it is difficult for the regulator to set the value of X correctly. If the X-factor is set too high, the firm might lose money, and perhaps even fold, leaving the government to pick up the pieces. If X is set

---

3. The design of a price cap is much more complex than our summary here. Interested readers should refer to Bernstein and Sappington (1999).

too low, the firm might earn excessive profits, which could be politically damaging.

Why Use Sophisticated Performance Measurement Methods?

The foregoing discussion revealed that correct measurement of potential productivity growth is crucial. Does this mean we need an entire book on the topic? We believe that such a book is indeed needed, because of the complexity of the topic and the importance of many details of its measurement for the effectiveness of the regulator in ensuring fair distribution of efficiency gains, whether arising from improvements in technology or simply from improvements in the management of a monopoly.

By way of illustration, consider the case of electricity distribution. What are the potential dangers in defining productivity using a traditional ratio measure, such as the volume of electricity supplied in kilowatt hours (kWh) per dollar of costs? In this case we could measure average annual productivity growth using the change in kWh/US$ over the past five years in the industry, and we could measure the relative efficiency of the firm by comparing its kWh/US$ with those of other firms in the industry.

Assume that we find that the industry's kWh/US$ has improved by 2 percent per year over the past five years and that the kWh/US$ of the firm is 20 percent below that of the best firm in the industry. Given this information, the regulator could set the X-factor at 6 percent per year for this firm, that is, the 2 percent expected of all firms in the industry, plus 20/5 = 4 percent in productivity catch-up to ensure that the firm has caught up with the best firm by the end of the five-year regulatory period.

This process seems quite easy, but it contains many traps for the unwary. For example, consider the following five issues:

- Do the firms differ in terms of average customer sizes and/or customer density? If so, the chosen productivity measure will not account for possible differences in output composition across firms.
- Are some firms larger than others and therefore able to achieve scale economies?
- Do input prices differ across years or across firms? It so, how has this been accounted for?
- Have the last five years been "typical"? For example, has the regulatory system changed recently? If so, could part of the past productivity growth be due to catch-up, which may not be achievable over the next five years?

- To what extent are all firms able to achieve the industry average level of productivity growth? If some distributors are located in areas with low population growth, are they likely to be less able to reap the productivity-enhancing benefits embedded in new capital investments?

These five issues are by no means an exhaustive list of possible problems, but they do illustrate some of the dangers that may result from the use of suboptimal productivity measures. The good news is that we can address many of these problems if we can get access to good quality data and if we use more sophisticated productivity measurement methods.

This is where this book comes in. Our aim is to outline the valuable information that you can obtain if you have access to good quality data. Thus in the early chapters we assume that we do have access to good quality data, and then illustrate the wealth of information that you can derive from the application of sophisticated productivity measurement methods. We then acknowledge the realities regulators in many developing and industrial countries face, and discuss how to proceed when data are limited in quality and quantity. We debate what you can do in this situation and use the good data case as a benchmark against which we can assess the problems that regulators may face when using second-best productivity information in setting price caps.

Some Performance Measurement Terminology

In this section we introduce some of the terminology used in performance measurement, and also briefly describe the main performance measurement methods. Box 2.1 summarizes all the information presented. For those who wish to learn more, the CRB book provides a comprehensive introduction to the terminology and the methodologies.

Productivity is the ratio of output over input. In the simple case when we have only one input and one output, this is an easy calculation. However, when we have more than one input and/or more than one output we need to use weights to construct an output index and an input index so as to allow the construction of a TFP index, which is equal to the ratio of the output index over the input index. We will discuss TFP index methods shortly, but first let us look at a one-input, one-output example.

Consider a simple example of five small water-carting firms in India, where the only input is labor and the only output is volume of water in kiloliters (kl) delivered per day by bucket. The sample data are listed in

Box 2.1. *Performance Measurement Terminology*

The *production frontier* (or production function) is a function, $y = f(x)$, that describes the maximum output, y, a firm can produce using any particular set of inputs, x. Production functions are usually estimated using sample data on a number of firms.

Technical efficiency (TE) is a firm's ability to achieve maximum output given its set of inputs. TE scores vary between 0 and 1. A value of 1 indicates full efficiency and operations are on the production frontier. A value of less than 1 reflects operations below the frontier. The wedge between 1 and the value observed measures technical inefficiency. This is an output-oriented TE measure. An input-oriented TE measure reflects the degree to which a firm that must produce a particular output level, y, could proportionally reduce its use of inputs and still remain within the feasible production set (that is, on or below the production frontier).

Technical change (TC) (or technological progress) is an increase in the maximum output that can be produced given an input vector, x, and is reflected in a shift in the production frontier over time. This is often slow for utilities and transport with the exception of the telecommunications sector, where progress has been, and continues to be, dramatic.

Scale efficiency (SE) is a measure of the degree to which a firm is optimizing the size of its operations. A firm can be too small or too large, resulting in a productivity penalty associated with not operating at the technically optimal scale of operation.

Input mix allocative efficiency (AE) is a firm's ability to select the correct mix of input quantities so as to ensure that the input price ratios equal the ratios of the corresponding marginal products, that is, the additional output obtained from an additional unit of input. The AE score varies between 0 and 1, with a value of 1 indicating full allocative efficiency. Most microeconomics textbook assume that all firms are technically efficient. In that special case full allocative efficiency equates to full cost efficiency or cost minimization.

Output mix allocative efficiency is a firm's ability to select the combination of outputs quantities in a way that ensures that the ratio of output prices equals the ratio of marginal costs, that is, the additional cost corresponding to the production of an additional unit of product. A firm that is technically efficient, scale efficient, and achieves input mix and output mix allocative efficiency, is maximizing profits for given input and output prices.

Total factor productivity is the ratio of output over input, y/x. When there is more than one input and/or output, this calculation requires weights to be specified. These weights are usually based on price information. The TFP of two firms facing the same operating environment at one point in time can differ because of TE, AE, or SE differences. TFP can vary over time because of changes in TE, AE, and SE, but also because of TC.

(Box continues on the following page.)

Box 2.1. *(continued)*

Cost efficiency (CE) is a firm's ability to produce a particular output, y, at minimum cost, given the input prices it faces. Note that CE = AE × TE, and hence that CE varies between 0 and 1, with a value of 1 indicating full cost efficiency.

Cost frontier (or cost function) is a function, $c = g(y, w)$, which relates the minimum cost, c, that is required to produce a particular output vector, y, given an input price vector, w. We can also estimate a variable cost frontier, $c_v = g(y, x_f, w_v)$, where c_v is variable costs, x_f is the quantities of those inputs assumed fixed in the short run, and w_v is the prices of variable inputs. The distance a firm is above the cost frontier reflects the CE of that firm, which may be due to AE and/or TE.

Distance function is a function, $d = h(x, y)$, that measures the efficiency wedge for a firm in a multi-input, multi-output production context. It is thus a generalization of the concept of the production frontier. A distance function can also take an input orientation or an output orientation.

---

table 2.1 and plotted in figure 2.1. The productivity ratio is calculated for each firm and reported in the final column of table 2.1. It shows that firm B is the most productive, delivering 1.67 kl of water per person, while firms C and D are the least productive, delivering 1 kl of water per person.

One way to visualize these productivity ratios on a diagram is to draw a line between the origin and each of the data points. These lines are depicted in figure 2.2. This line will have a slope equal to the ratio of output

Table 2.1. *Data for Water-Carting Example*
(input = labor, output = kl)

Firm	Input (x)	Output (y)	Productivity (y/x)
A	5	7	1.40
B	3	5	1.67
C	1	1	1.00
D	2	2	1.00
E	5	6	1.20

Source: Authors (for this and all other tables and figures throughout the book).

Figure 2.1. *Graphic Illustration of Data for Water-Carting Example*

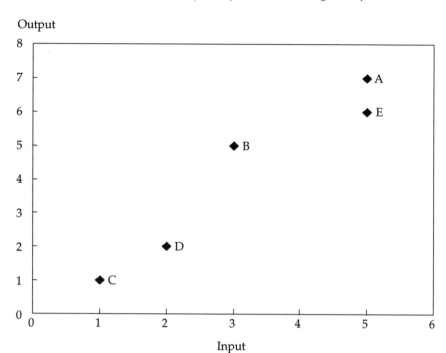

over input, that is, the slope of the line reflects the productivity of the firm. A steeper line indicates higher productivity. Observe that firm B has the steepest line and firms C and D have the line with the smallest slope.

A production frontier is a function that represents the maximum output that can be produced using a given amount of input. That is, it represents best-practice performance in the industry. Production frontiers are usually estimated using sample data on the inputs and outputs used by a number of firms. Frontiers can be constructed using data on firms that have many inputs and/or many outputs. The two methods that are most often used to construct frontiers are data envelopment analysis (DEA) and stochastic frontier analysis (SFA). We will define these methods shortly, but first let us look at a simple one-input, one-output example.

Consider the sample data depicted in figure 2.1. We can construct a DEA frontier over this simple data by using a pencil and ruler. This production frontier is depicted in figure 2.3. Note that when we have more inputs and/or more outputs we need to use a computer to construct the

Figure 2.2. *Productivity Ratios for Water-Carting Example*

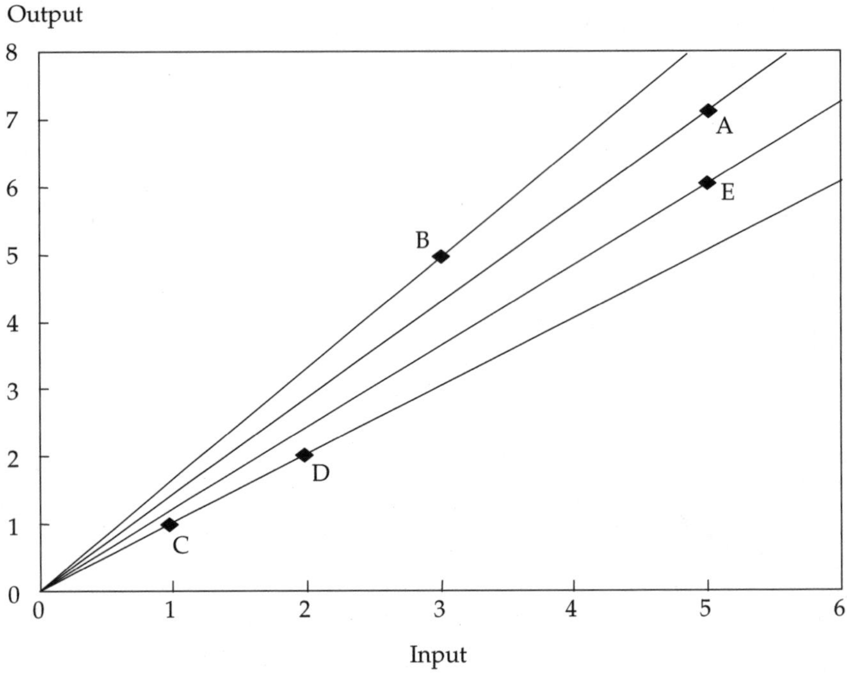

Output

Input

frontier. In figure 2.3 firms A, B, and C are used to construct the frontier, and the other two firms, D and E, lie below the frontier.[4]

The distance between the data point and the frontier determines the TE of the firm. For example, firm E in figure 2.3 could potentially increase its output up to the frontier (at point A). Hence we define the TE of firm E as being equal to the ratio of what it is producing (6 kl) over what it could potentially produce (7 kl), given its current level of inputs (5 laborers). Thus for firm E, TE = 6/7 = 0.86, that is, it is producing 86 percent of its potential output.[5] The TE of the frontier firms in figure 2.3 (firms A, B, and C) is

---

4. Standard production functions are usually fitted using regression methods. These regression methods fit a line through the center of the data, and hence measure average practice. Frontier methods, by contrast, fit a surface over the data, and hence measure best practice.

5. This measure of TE is called output-oriented, because it asks by how much the firm could increase its output given its level of inputs. Alternatively, one can

Figure 2.3. *A Production Frontier*

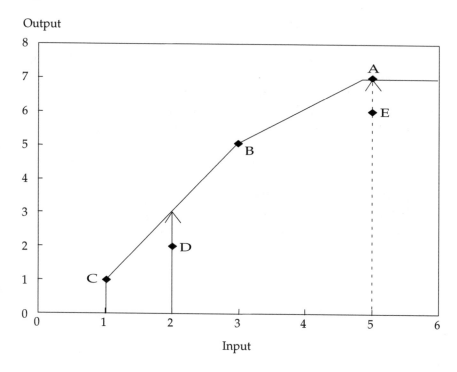

Output

Input

equal to 1. This is because they define the frontier. The TE of firm D is equal to $2/3 = 0.67$, that is, firm D is producing 67 percent of its potential output.

Note that firms A, B, and C are all fully efficient in terms of TE, while when we looked at the productivity ratios earlier we saw that firms A and C had lower productivity than firm B. Indeed, firm C had the lowest productivity in the sample. How can this be? The reason is that TE is only one part of productivity. Another component of productivity is SE. SE reflects the fact that there is usually an optimal firm size, and not all firms operate at the optimal size. For example, large firms may be more productive than

define input-oriented TE, which asks how much the firm could reduce its inputs given its level of output. The two measures generally produce quite similar TE scores. The input-oriented measure is most often used in network industries, like water and electricity, because the firm is usually required to supply a particular level of service to the community. Hence a request for an increase in output is not very sensible.

small firms because they can have labor teams that specialize in particular tasks.

To measure scale efficiency we must construct an additional frontier on figure 2.3, namely, a constant returns to scale (CRS) frontier. This is a frontier that allows firms of any size to be benchmarked against each other, for example, small firms can be benchmarked against big firms and vice versa. The frontier that we have already drawn in figure 2.3 is known as a variable returns to scale (VRS) frontier. This VRS frontier was constructed so that small firms are benchmarked against small firms and big firms against big firms.

A VRS frontier and a CRS frontier are drawn in figure 2.4. In this simple example, the CRS frontier is simply equal to the line from the origin through the point defined by firm B. Firm B is chosen because it has the largest productivity. The distance between each data point and the CRS frontier is called TE_{CRS}. This measure of efficiency will contain both TE and SE. For example, consider firm D in figure 2.4. It has $TE_{CRS} = 2/3.33 = 0.6$. The gap

Figure 2.4. *CRS and VRS Production Frontiers*

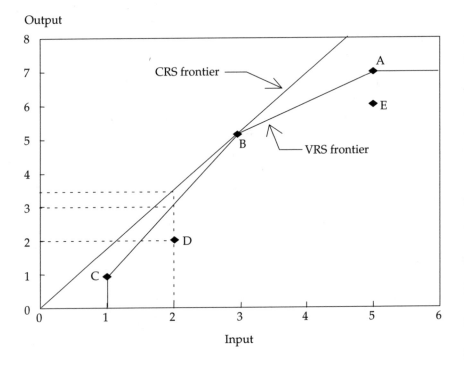

between the CRS and VRS frontier provides a measure of the SE of firm D. It is able to increase output from 3 kl (on the VRS frontier) up to 3.33 kl on the CRS frontier, thus its SE = $3/3.33 = 0.9$. This implies that firm D could improve its efficiency by approximately 10 percent if it were to increase its scale of operation to the optimal scale of operation (as defined by firm B).

Thus for firm D we have found that TE = 0.67, SE = 0.9, and $TE_{CRS} = 0.6$. Note that $TE_{CRS} = TE \times SE$. That is, $0.6 = 0.67 \times 0.9$. This is always true. Table 2.2 reports the efficiency scores of all five firms .

Furthermore, if we take the productivity ratios reported in table 2.1 and divide each productivity ratio by the largest productivity ratio in the sample (the firm B ratio of 1.67) we obtain the TE_{CRS} scores. For example, if we take the productivity ratio of firm D (1.00) and divide it by 1.67, we obtain 0.6, which is the TE_{CRS} score of firm D. Thus in this simple example we can see that the productivity of firms can differ for two reasons: technical efficiency and scale efficiency.

This information is particularly interesting to regulators of network firms. For example, when setting the X-factor for a particular firm, say firm D, the regulator will usually want to remove the effects of scale efficiency from the productivity measures. This is because the firm generally has no control over its scale of operation, which is usually determined by historical factors. Thus most regulators tend to focus on measures of technical efficiency (from a VRS frontier) when setting firm-specific X-factors. The regulator does not want to disadvantage a firm for not being the optimal size when the firm has no control over its size.[6]

Table 2.2. *Efficiency Scores for Water-Carting Example*

Firm	TE	SE	TE_{CRS}
A	1.00	0.84	0.84
B	1.00	1.00	1.00
C	1.00	0.60	0.60
D	0.67	0.90	0.60
E	0.86	0.84	0.72

6. This discussion assumes that firms are not permitted to amalgamate or split up into smaller firms. Over the longer term, a regulator may use scale efficiency information to make some recommendations in this area.

The discussion thus far has used a simple one-input, one-output example. If we consider the more general case of multiple-inputs and/or multiple-outputs, we are required to measure productivity as the ratio of an output index divided by an input index. The input index is generally defined as a weighted sum of all inputs, and the output index is a weighted sum of all outputs.

$$\text{TFP} = \frac{\text{output index}}{\text{input index}}.$$

The weights used in these indexes are usually cost shares in the input index and revenue shares in the output index, that is, we use price information. These price-based index number (PIN) methods are described in detail in the next chapter. Note that the index number formula most commonly used in TFP calculations is the Törnqvist index (defined in chapter 3).

When we have multiple inputs and multiple outputs we find that TFP can now differ between firms for four reasons:

- Technical efficiency
- Scale efficiency
- Input mix allocative efficiency
- Output mix allocative efficiency.

Input mix allocative efficiency relates to the notion that the firm is trying to produce its output using the least-cost mix of inputs, given the input prices the firm faces. For example, if the price of capital falls relative to the price of labor, the firm may be able to reduce its costs by using less labor and more capital, for instance, by introducing a new computerized billing system.

Output mix allocative efficiency relates to the notion that the firm is trying to produce the optimal mix of outputs given the output prices the firm face. For example, if the price of sewerage removal rises relative to the price of water supply, one of the Indian water-carting firms we used in our earlier example may be able to increase its revenues by delivering less water and removing more sewerage without changing the amount of inputs used.

When setting firm-specific X-factors, a regulator will often want to remove these allocative efficiency factors from the performance comparisons between firms. The regulator may wish to remove the input mix allocative efficiency component because the capital intensity of network firms is often largely determined by population density. Furthermore, the output mix allocative efficiency component is often removed because network firms rarely have the ability to alter their output mix, for instance, a mix of large and small customers.

Hence in setting the firm-specific part of the X-factors, regulators tend to focus primarily on measures of technical efficiency. This is not an absolute rule, but it is generally the case. Note also that this is a conservative approach. If the regulator included allocative efficiency (or scale efficiency) in the X-factor calculations, the X-factor could only rise.

The foregoing discussion relates to comparisons of the TFP of two or more firms at one point in time. When we wish to compare the TFP of a firm or an industry over time, an additional factor can contribute to TFP growth, namely, technical change. Technical change can be represented by an upward shift in the production frontier over time. It could, for example, be the result of the development of new technology, such as new equipment for cleaning and re-lining old pipes in a water supply firm.

A number of authors refer to technical change as a frontier-shift and to technical efficiency change, that is, getting closer to the frontier, as catch-up.

To summarize, TFP growth over time could be the result of five factors as follows:

- Technical change (frontier shift)
- Technical efficiency change (catch-up)
- Scale efficiency change
- Input mix allocative efficiency change
- Output mix allocative efficiency change.

When setting X-factors, a regulator generally wants to ask the frontier firms to achieve an annual productivity improvement equal to the historical level of technical change (frontier shift), and wishes to ask the inefficient firms (those below the frontier) to achieve this plus some technical efficiency improvement (catch-up).

In most cases the regulator will use price-based TFP indexes to measure TFP change in the industry over the last 5 or 10 years, and then use this TFP change measure as an estimate of the likely future rate of technical change in the industry. This is generally a reasonable measure, but this is not always the case. For example, during a period following a change in regulatory structure, the new incentives may have encouraged a number of inefficient firms to catch up to the better firms. In this case the industry-level TFP change measure could be 3 percent per year, with 1 percent resulting from technical efficiency change (catch-up) and 2 percent from technical change (frontier shift). Now if the regulator uses the 3 percent measure as a measure of potential technical change, the frontier firms will be asked to do too much.

This brings us to an important point: price-based TFP index numbers measure TFP, but they cannot be used to decompose TFP into the foregoing components. You need an estimate of the technology (the production frontier) to be able to decompose TFP into components. This is one of the main disadvantages of TFP index numbers; however, index numbers do have the advantage that they only require data on two observations, for instance, two firms, while frontier methods require data on a large number of firms.

Two main approaches are used to construct production frontiers, DEA and SFA. For both methods we require data on the input and output quantities used by a sample of firms. We then fit a frontier over the top of these data points and measure technical inefficiency as the distance between each data point and the estimated frontier. DEA uses linear programming methods to construct the frontier, while SFA uses methods similar to regression methods, but more complex.

The two methods have various advantages and disadvantages. SFA has the advantage that it attempts to account for the effects of data noise (data errors, omitted variables, and so on), while DEA assumes the data are free of noise. SFA has the second advantage that you can use standard statistical tests such as t-tests to test the significance of variables included in the model, while DEA does not allow this. However, DEA has the advantage that you do not need to specify a functional form for the production frontier, while in SFA you must select a functional form, for example, logarithmic. Another advantage of DEA is that it is easier to calculate using available software than SFA.

Overall, both methods have their merits. If possible, using both methods as a sensitivity test is wise, and generally they should produce similar results.[7] In regulation, DEA has been the more popular method, probably because DEA methods are easy to draw on diagrams, easy to calculate, and until recently SFA could not accommodate multiple outputs.[8]

---

7. For an example of a study that applied a number of methods to one dataset see Carrington, Coelli, and Groom (2002), who applied DEA, SFA and corrected ordinary least squares to data on Australian and U.S. gas distributors for the purpose of setting price caps.

8. SFA methods can now easily accommodate multiple outputs using a multi-output production function known as a distance function.

This chapter has introduced a good deal of terminology. To help summarize this information we provide two summaries. Box 2.1 provided informal definitions of some of the performance measurement terminology commonly used in regulatory debates, such as efficiency and technical change, and can be used for reference. Table 2.3 compares the key characteristics of the three main performance measurement methods: price-based index number (PIN), SFA, and DEA.

Summing Up

In this chapter we described an example of a situation where a regulator wishes to set price caps for electricity distribution firms and discussed the possible pitfalls of using simple performance measures. We then outlined the types of information that can be derived from the use of more sophisticated performance measurement methods. In particular, we discussed how productivity differences between firms could be decomposed into various components, including technical efficiency, scale efficiency, and allocative efficiency, and how productivity changes over time can be decomposed into technical change (frontier shift), technical efficiency change (catch-up), scale efficiency change, and allocative efficiency change.

In many instances a regulator can benefit from having access to this richer information. For example, consider the case where a regulator has information on productivity differences between firms, but has no information on the contribution of scale efficiency in these differences. There is a danger that the regulator could set unachievable productivity targets on the small firms if they face scale diseconomies.

Alternatively, consider the case where a regulator has obtained a measure of industry productivity growth over the last five years of 5 percent per year, but has no information on the contribution of technical change (frontier shift) in this figure. If part of the productivity growth, say 2 percent, was due to technical efficiency change (catch-up) derived from a change in regulatory regime, and hence only 3 percent was due to technical change (frontier shift), then a request for 5 percent productivity growth over the next five years may be too high if little scope remains for continuing catch-up over the next five years.[9]

---

9. For a change in regulatory regime to induce this type of catch-up effect is not unusual. For example, consider the case of the U.K. electricity industry, which achieved substantial growth in productivity in the period following the change to price cap regulation.

Table 2.3. *A Comparison of the Main Approaches to Efficiency and Productivity Measurement*

Category	Price-based index numbers (PIN)	Stochastic frontier analysis (SFA)[a]	Data envelopment analysis (DEA)
Description	Traditional index numbers approach to TFP measurement. Prices are used as the weights. Törnqvist or Fisher formulas are usually employed. The Elteto and Koves (1964) and Szulc (1964) transformation is generally applied to cross-sectional data to ensure the transitivity of multilateral comparisons.	An econometric method that estimates a production frontier of the form: $y = f(x) + v - u$, where y is the output, $f(x)$ are all the inputs, v is an error term capturing unpredictable perturbations and u captures technical inefficiency. A cost frontier (short run or long run) or a distance function can be used instead.	A linear programming method that constructs a nonparametric production frontier by fitting a piece-wise linear surface over the data points.
Data needs	Quantity and price data on inputs and outputs for two or more firms or time periods.	For a production frontier or distance function: quantity data on inputs and outputs for a sample of firms, ideally over a number of years. For a long-run cost frontier: total costs, input prices, and output quantities. For a short-run cost frontier: variable costs, variable input prices, and fixed input quantities and output quantities.	Quantity data on inputs and outputs for a sample of firms, ideally over a number of years. However, if price data are available, you can also use it to calculate allocative efficiency.

Advantages	Can do a study with only two observations.	Attempts to account for noise.	Identifies a set of peer firms (efficient firms with similar input and output mixes) for each inefficient firm.
	Is reproducible and transparent.	Environmental variables are easier to deal with.	Can easily handle multiple outputs.
	Captures allocative efficiency.	Allows for the conduct of traditional statistical tests of hypotheses.	Does not assume a functional form for the frontier or a distributional form for the inefficiency error term.
		Easier to identify outliers.	
		Cost frontier and distance function can deal with multiple outputs.	
Drawbacks	Need price information.	The decomposition of the error term into noise and efficiency components may be affected by the particular distributional forms specified and by the related assumption that error skewness is an indication of inefficiency.	May be influenced by noise.
	Cannot decompose TFP measure into components.		Traditional hypothesis tests are not possible.[b]
		Requires large sample size for robust estimates, which may not be available early on in the life of a regulator.	Requires large sample size for robust estimates, which may not be available early on in the life of a regulator

a. Ordinary least squares (OLS) estimation of a frontier can be viewed as a special case of SFA, where one assumes that there is no inefficiency. Corrected OLS estimation, where the OLS intercept is shifted so that the frontier envelopes all data points, is also a special case of SFA where one assumes that there is no noise.

b. This drawback may be limited using bootstrapping techniques as proposed by Simar and Wilson (2000).

These two examples illustrate how the use of sophisticated performance measurement methods can help regulators make better-informed decisions. However, these sophisticated methods require access to good quality data. In the following two chapters we will assume that we have access to good quality data and outline how to measure and decompose productivity change using a number of alternative approaches. In later chapters we will relax the good data assumption and discuss some of the available options.

3

Some TFP Measurement and Decomposition Methods

We begin this chapter by noting that it involves much technical discussion of how to measure TFP and how to decompose these TFP measures into components that are of interest to regulators. This chapter assumes that we have access to good quality data, an assumption that is relaxed in later chapters.

As noted in chapter 2, the definition of TFP is intuitively quite simple. It tells the regulator how much output is achieved with each unit of input, which would seem to be a reasonable performance indicator for most situations a regulator has to face. In other words, it is equal to the ratio of output over input, and when there is only one output (Y_1) and one input (X_1), it boils down to the following expression:

$$\text{TFP} = Y_1/X_1. \tag{3.1}$$

This formula is, however, too simple in practice, because most operators tend to rely on a combination of inputs, for instance, labor, capital, and others, that can have varying relative importance across firms. Moreover, many regulated industries offer multiple outputs as well. For instance, an airport, port, or rail operator will often cater to both freight and passengers. A water company can produce water, distribute it, collect raw sewerage, and treat the sewerage, which are all separate products. Telecommunications operators often offer both local and long distance services and many fixed operators are diversifying into mobile telephony. Moreover, the latest trend in the sector is to have multi-utility operators. Many electricity

operators are crossing over to telecommunications and the main international actors in the water sector are following. This suggests that a reasonable measure of TFP generally needs to take into account M outputs and K
inputs, where M and K are usually both larger than one.

As noted in chapter 2, a TFP index is generally constructed as the ratio
of an output index to an input index. For example, we could use a linear
weighting function to define a TFP index as

$$\text{TFP} = \sum_{m=1}^{M} a_m Y_m \bigg/ \sum_{k=1}^{K} b_k X_k, \tag{3.2}$$

where a_m and b_k are weights that reflect the relative importance of the various inputs and outputs.

Two questions follow directly from equation (3.2). First, how do we select the values for the weights? Second, is a linear function appropriate or
should we choose another mathematical form? The issue of the appropriate mathematical form to choose will be dealt with later in this chapter. At
this point we will focus on the weights issue. There are two natural choices:
market prices and shadow prices.

Market prices are the prices that people must pay for the goods or services. For example, consider the case of a water supply firm. Some relevant
input prices could be the wage rate per hour for labor and the rental price
per hour for a computer. Some relevant output prices could be the price
per liter for water supply and the price per day of sewerage connection.

Shadow prices, by contrast, are derived from the shape of the underlying production technology (or frontier), and are usually expressed in ratio
form. For example, the ratio of the shadow price of labor to the shadow
price of computers would reflect the degree to which an hour of labor can
be substituted with some quantity of computer hours (with output levels
held constant). In economics jargon this reflects the marginal rate of technical substitution between the inputs. Similarly, the ratio of the shadow price
of water supply to the shadow price of sewerage services would reflect the
degree to which a liter of water supply can be substituted with some quantity of sewerage services (with input levels held constant). In economics
jargon this reflects the marginal rate of technical transformation between
the outputs.

Under conditions of perfect competition, shadow prices and market
prices will be equal. If they are not equal, we say that a certain amount of
input mix or output mix allocative inefficiency exists. However, we need to

be careful here, because if the market prices are in some way distorted, for example, because of a regulatory or political intervention, the issue of allocative inefficiency is less clear.

The methods used to measure TFP can be divided into two groups according to the types of prices employed, that is, market or shadow prices. In chapter 2 we introduced three groups of methods (table 2.3):

- Price-based index numbers
- Stochastic frontier analysis
- Data envelopment analysis.

Essentially, PIN methods use market prices, while SFA and DEA methods involve the estimation of a production technology (frontier), and hence the use of shadow prices derived from the shape of the estimated frontier.

In the remainder of this chapter we provide a detailed description of how to use these methods to measure TFP growth. We also describe how you can use the frontier methods (SFA and DEA) to decompose the measured TFP growth into components that are of interest to regulators.

Price-Based Index Numbers

PIN is the sensible choice when few data are available. To make a performance assessment the regulator only needs to obtain comparable information on outputs and inputs for two points in time: the base period or period 0, say the first year in which a price cap prevails, and the end of period or period 1, possibly the year before the cap revision is due. Once this data problem has been resolved, the only outstanding issue is to select the weights. A natural choice for the weights in our TFP index is to select the market prices of the inputs and the outputs.[1] Using equation (3.2), the TFP change from period 0 to period 1 can be written as the ratio

$$\mathrm{TFP}_1 / \mathrm{TFP}_0 = \left[\sum_{m=1}^{M} a_m Y_{m1} \Big/ \sum_{k=1}^{K} b_k X_{k1} \Big/ \sum_{m=1}^{M} a_m Y_{m0} \Big/ \sum_{k=1}^{K} b_k X_{k0} \right]. \tag{3.3}$$

This expression assumes that the weights are the same in the two periods. However, the prices may vary between the two periods. Which set should we use, base period prices or end of period prices?

---

1. Note that if we refer to prices without including a prefix such as market or shadow, assume that we are referring to market prices.

Using the base period prices yields a TFP index, which is the ratio of a Laspeyres output quantity index to a Laspeyres input quantity index. Using period 1 prices (assuming that this is the end of period) yields a Paasche index. Many regulators would see this choice as arbitrary and prefer to rely on the geometric mean of these two indexes, which is known as the Fisher index.[2] A popular alternative in recent publications on TFP measures in privatized industries, which provides nearly identical results, is the Törnqvist index, which implies an underlying translog technology.

The log form of the Törnqvist TFP change index between periods 0 and 1, is defined as

$$\ln{(TFP_{n1}/TFP_{n0})}^T = 0.5 \sum_{j=1}^{M} \left[(r_{jn1} + r_{jn0}) \cdot (y_{jn1} - y_{jn0}) \right]$$
$$- 0.5 \sum_{i=1}^{K} \left[(s_{in1} + s_{in0}) \cdot (x_{in1} - x_{in0}) \right], \tag{3.4}$$

where the T superscript refers to Törnqvist, x_{jnt} and y_{jnt} are, respectively, the log of the j-th input and output of the n-th firm in the t-th time period, and s_{jnt} (r_{jnt}) is the cost (revenue) share of the j-th input (output) for the n-th firm in the t-th time period.[3] In sum, with information on the physical quantity of inputs and outputs and with information provided by balance sheets on cost and revenue shares of each input and output, a regulator can make a fair quantitative assessment of the TFP evolution of any operator.

The main problems with these indexes is that they assume that the regulator has a lot of information on the actual physical quantities of outputs and inputs. Regulators generally have a good deal of physical data on outputs, that is, volume of freight, number of passengers, number of kilowatt hours of electricity, liters of water, or number of successful telephone calls.

---

2. This Fisher index has a number of useful properties. In particular, it implies an underlying quadratic production technology, which is much more sensible, that is, more flexible, from an economic theory point of view than the linear production technologies that are implicit in the Laspeyres and Paasche indexes.

3. For further discussion of these various price-based index number options see chapters 4 and 5 in CRB. Also see Diewert (2000), who argues convincingly that direct and indirect Fisher and Törnqvist indexes provide ideal measures of TFP when one looks at the test or axiomatic approach to index number evaluation. Furthermore, when comparing two firms at one point in time one needs to make a transitivity adjustment to Törnqvist or Fisher indexes. These are detailed in chapter 4 in CRB.

They generally have much less physical data on inputs. Indeed, unless they are required to provide the information, operators will seldom volunteer the physical measure of inputs such as energy consumption. This limited data on quantity pushes the regulator to use as much as possible the information available in balance sheets, that is, cost and revenue data from annual reports. This can be frustrating, as little detailed breakdown of this information is generally available unless the regulator has managed to impose strict regulatory accounting rules on the operators. In this respect the Office of Water Services in the United Kingdom is a leader in the field (see www.open.gov.uk/ofwat).

One solution in that type of situation is to rely on an indirect TFP index. This indirect index is defined by deflating total revenue and total costs by suitable price indexes to obtain quantity indexes. That is, because price × quantity = value, then quantity = value/price. One can then define TFP as the ratio of deflated revenue over deflated cost.[4] This is also an approximation, because often the price indexes that are used for deflating are imperfect, as discussed later. They are probably compiled for the industry by a central statistical agency. Recognizing these constraints is crucial, because they may introduce biases into the TFP measurements.

To see how these biases could occur in practice, consider the case of a railways performance study. The best input price index available might be that defined for public transport industries in general, while the output price index may be defined for the rail industry alone. These price indexes would most likely be Laspeyres indexes, that is, based on base period weights, and would also be calculated using quantity weights for the whole industry. Hence if the input mix and/or output mix of a particular firm differs substantially from the average mixes in the industry, for example, if a firm uses a lower proportion of labor to capital or provides a higher proportion of freight to passenger services, the deflated revenue and/or cost figures for this firm may not provide a reasonable approximation to the required quantity indexes. Thus the resulting TFP index for this firm may be misleading.

How misleading can this be? Imagine a case where the ratio of passenger to freight services is 4 to 1 in the industry in terms of revenue, but firm

---

4. Once again, the form of the price index formula used (Laspeyres, Paasche, Törnqvist, or Fisher) will imply a particular functional form for the underlying production technology. Laspeyres and Paasche will imply restrictive first-order forms, while Törnqvist and Fisher imply more flexible second-order functional forms.

A has a ratio of 1 to 4 (we assume all firms face the same prices). If the price of passenger services increases by 10 percent between two periods while the other prices and all quantities remain constant, the output price index for the industry will increase by 8 percent, while the true price index firm A faces will only increase by 2 percent. However, the revenue of firm A, which increases by 2 percent, will be deflated by the industry price index, which increases by 8 percent, which will suggest that the real output of firm A has fallen, when in reality it has not.[5]

In sum, the PINs can be useful to many regulators with only limited databases, but as with any index, understanding the instrument's limitations is a requirement for ensuring the credibility of its regulatory uses. A necessary condition for its effective use is a good understanding of what each price indicator hides and the extent to which average price applies or does not apply to any individual operator.

PIN methods have the advantage that they can be used when you only have access to data on one firm or a few firms, or you only have access to industry-level data; however, they have the disadvantage that you cannot use PIN methods to decompose TFP change into components, such as technical change (frontier shift) and technical efficiency change (catch-up). In the following sections we assume that we have access to panel data on a number of firms, that is, we have data on N firms over T time periods, for example, we could have annual data on $N = 40$ firms over $T = 8$ years. Given access to this type of data, we can use frontier methods such as SFA and DEA to measure and decompose TFP growth.

Production Frontiers, Single Output Case

For the sake of simplicity, we focus first on the standard single output production process, and leave the discussion of the multiple output case for later. This discussion is quite relevant in practice, as many regulators tend to treat the firms they monitor as single output producers and rely on a

---

5. These types of issues are also important to keep in mind as we discuss production and cost frontier approaches to TFP measurement, because our quantity data often come in the form of deflated value measures. In many cases the prices we use may be questionable. First, they may be measured with error. Second, they may be measured well, but some prices may be distorted by regulatory and other factors, for example, a government-owned utility might set electricity prices below cost. Third, the market prices may be measured well, but they may not reflect society's priorities, for instance, this may be revealed in divergences between the market price and shadow price of labor in government-owned firms where the government and society put a value on high employment levels.

constant price valuation of the operator's revenue as an approximation of this output.

The TFP change (TFPC) measures derived from a production frontier can be decomposed into three components: technical efficiency change (TEC), technical change (TC), and scale efficiency change (SEC). This decomposition is multiplicative, that is,

$$\text{TFPC} = \text{TEC} \times \text{TC} \times \text{SEC}.$$

Note that allocative efficiency does not appear in this decomposition. This is because the TFP measures derived from production frontiers do not include this factor; however, allocative efficiency does come into play when we consider cost frontiers.

When implementing this simple approach, the first question to address is the choice of functional form. The Cobb-Douglas is a relatively simple functional form. For the case when we have one output (Y) and three input variables (X_1 = capital, X_2 = labor, and X_3 = other inputs), the Cobb-Douglas production function has the form

$$Y = a_0 X_1^{\alpha_1} X_2^{\alpha_2} X_3^{\alpha_3}, \tag{3.4a}$$

where α_0, α_1, α_2, and α_3 are unknown parameters to be estimated. The Cobb-Douglas is popular largely because the logarithm of equation (3.4a) produces a function that is linear in parameters, and is therefore easy to estimate using standard linear regression methods. The logarithm of equation (3.4a) is

$$y = \alpha_0 + \alpha_1 x_1 + \alpha_2 x_2 + \alpha_3 x_3, \tag{3.4b}$$

where $\alpha_0 = \log(a_0)$ and $x_i = \log(X_i)$. Note that α_1, α_2, and α_3 are the elasticities of output with respect to capital, labor, and other, respectively. A clear advantage of this functional form is that it only requires the estimation of four parameters, which can be done with relatively small data samples. It is convenient, and this may be why it was so commonly used in the early literature on efficiency and continues to be contrasted with more flexible forms in recent literature. However, from the viewpoint of most regulators, it is likely to be too restrictive. The Cobb-Douglas assumes that all firms have the same production elasticities, the same scale elasticities, and unitary elasticities of substitution, which is quite restrictive for most studies trying to compare regulated operators.

One additional advantage of the Cobb-Douglas may be that its analytical expression is simple enough to allow the derivation of the cost frontier from the estimation of the production frontier or vice versa. This is quite useful when a regulator can only rely on total cost data from balance sheets. It is, however, quite problematic conceptually, as most of the analytical work underlying the duality between production and cost frontiers assumes perfectly competitive markets, which is rarely the norm among regulated industries. They are regulated because they are not strictly competitive.[6] Because of this, it is often safer to use a production frontier if you have access to suitable data.

Given the restricted nature of the Cobb-Douglas, regulators will generally need to seek out a more flexible functional form, irrespective of whether they decide to estimate a cost or a production frontier. Currently the most commonly used flexible functional form is the translog functional form. While it requires the estimation of many more parameters than the Cobb-Douglas, it does not impose the restrictions imposed by the Cobb-Douglas, and is therefore generally preferable, unless a hypothesis test justifies the Cobb-Douglas restrictions or data limitations preclude the use of the translog. A translog stochastic production frontier may be defined as[7]

$$y_{nt} = \alpha_0 + \sum_{i=1}^{K} \alpha_i x_{int} + 0.5 \sum_{i=1}^{K} \sum_{j=1}^{K} \alpha_{ij} x_{int} x_{jnt} + \sum_{i=1}^{K} \delta_i x_{int} t + \lambda_1 t + 0.5 \lambda_{11} t^2 + v_{nt} - u_{nt},$$

$$n = 1, 2, \ldots, N; \; t = 1, 2, \ldots, T, \tag{3.5}$$

where y_{nt} is the log of output quantity; x_{int} is the log of i-th input quantity; t is a time trend; v_{nt} is a noise error term that picks up whatever the model could not explain; u_{nt} is the inefficiency term, entered with a negative sign because inefficiency means less output; and the Greek letters represent

---

6. See Schmidt and Lovell (1979) for an example of direct estimation of the cost frontier applied to electricity supply, and see Bravo-Ureta and Rieger (1991) for an example involving direct estimation of the production frontier applied to agriculture. In the latter case, a criticism of possible simultaneous equations bias could be leveled given that the inputs, which are assumed to be decision variables, appear as regressors in the production frontier. Schmidt and Lovell (1979) also consider the case where the production frontier is estimated simultaneously with the first-order conditions for cost minimization. They use maximum likelihood methods to estimate this system of equations, assuming that inputs are endogenous and outputs are exogenous. They consider two forms of this latter model, one where the average firm is assumed to be allocatively efficient and one where systematic deviation from allocative efficiency is permitted, for example, caused by a regulatory effect such as the Averch-Johnson effect.

7. In this and all other translog function in this book, symmetry is implicit, that is, $\alpha_{ij} = \alpha_{ji}$, etc.

unknown parameters to be estimated.[8] The subscripts n and t index firm and time period, respectively. As is also quite common, in this model we have used a time trend, t, to approximate technical change. While other possibilities exist, such as the use of annual dummy variables, the time trend approach is the most often used.[9]

A useful trick practitioners use that deserves consideration by most regulators is transforming the data so as to allow direct interpretation of the first-order translog parameters (the α_is) as the elasticities evaluated at the sample means.[10] This is done by ensuring that the arithmetic sample averages of the logged variables are 0, which is equivalent to setting the geometric means of the original (unlogged) data equal to 1. Essentially it consists of dividing every series by its geometric average. This will not change the results obtained, but is simply a convenient change in units of measurement.

The next stage is the actual calculation of the TFPC for each firm between any two time periods using estimates of the production frontier. Following Orea (2002),[11] the log of the TFPC between period $t = 0$ and $t = 1$, for the n-th firm can be defined to being equal to

$$
\ln\left(TFP_{n1} / TFP_{n0}\right) = \ln\left(TE_{n1} / TE_{n0}\right) + 0.5\left[(\partial y_{n0}/\partial t) + (\partial y_{n1}/\partial t)\right]
$$
$$
+ 0.5\sum_{k=1}^{K}\left[(SF_{n0}\,e_{kn0} + SF_{n1}\,e_{kn1})\cdot(x_{kn1} - x_{kn0})\right],
\tag{3.6}
$$

---

8. Those more statistically inclined should note that the most common assumptions are that the error terms, v_{nt} and u_{nt}, could take many different possible structures. The first is symmetrically distributed while the second is one-sided. Generally they are assumed to be independently and identically distributed as $N(0, \sigma_v^2)$ and $|N(0, \sigma_u^2)|$ random variables, respectively (see chapters 8 and 9 in CRB for further discussion).

9. In addition to this general specification, there is the need to ensure that the sum of the weights in the TFP measure adds up to 1. If the production elasticities from the estimated production frontier do not add up to 1, the literature usually picks either one of the following two choices. The first is to impose constant returns to scale on the production technology, but this will generally not be satisfactory in regulated industries, which are often considered to be natural monopolies with clear economies of scale. The second is to assume variable returns to scale and ensure that an appropriate scale efficiency change measure is included in the final TFP calculations, as suggested in Balk (1999); Kumbhakar and Lovell (2000); and Orea (2002). Most regulators will generally favor this approach.

10. If you do use scaled data to estimate the frontier, then you must be sure to use scaled data to calculate TFP, and so on, otherwise you will obtain incorrect results.

11. The two main approaches to TFP decomposition are the total differential approach (see, for example, Bauer 1990; Kumbhakar and Lovell 2000) and the index

where the three terms on the right-hand-side of equation (3.6) are the TEC, TC, and SEC terms, respectively. The technical efficiency measure, TE_{nt}, is the technical efficiency prediction of the n-th firm in the t-th time period obtained from equation (3.5).[12] The technical change measure is the mean of the technical change measures evaluated at the period 0 and period 1 data points, and can also be derived directly from the coefficients estimated for equation (3.5). The change in scale efficiency requires calculating the production elasticities from the parameters estimated for equation (3.5),[13] that is, you must calculate

$$e_{knt} = \partial y_{nt} / \partial x_{knt} = \alpha_k + \sum_{i=1}^{K} \alpha_{ki} x_{int} + \delta_k t \tag{3.7}$$

for each input at each data point, and also calculate the scale factors $SF_{nt} = (e_{nt} - 1)/e_{nt}$ at each data point, where $e_{nt} = \sum_{k=1}^{K} e_{knt}$ is the standard returns to scale elasticity.[14]

The TC measure requires calculating the partial derivative with respect to time at each data point. For firm n in period t this is

$$\partial y_{nt} / \partial t = \lambda_1 + \lambda_{11} t + \sum_{k=1}^{K} \delta_k x_{knt} . \tag{3.8}$$

---

number approach (see, for example, Caves, Christensen, and Diewert 1982a,b; Orea 2002), which exploits the translog identity. The two approaches result in almost identical formulas, the only differences being that the latter approach evaluates derivatives at both data points, while the first method chooses just one data point for derivative evaluation. Diewert (2000) argues in favor of the index number approach, because the total differential approach is an approximation to a continuous time measure, which can take many values. Thus in this book we use the index number approach; however, we do note that in most cases the two approaches will provide quite similar estimates.

12. Analytically, the TE is equal to the conditional expectation of $\exp(-u_{nt})$, given the value of $(v_{nt} - u_{nt})$. These measures are routinely reported by the statistical packages available to assess efficiency, such as the FRONTIER program by Coelli (1996b). This software can be downloaded from www.uq.edu.au/economics/staff/coelli.htm.

13. To be precise, the SEC measures derived from SFA frontiers in this book are not pure measures of scale efficiency change. First, it is possible that the measures obtained may also include the effects of scale-biased technical change, if this has occurred; however, this distinction is not something that regulators should be greatly concerned about. Second, as stated by Orea (2002 p. 12), this term "evaluates the contribution of non-constant returns to scale on productivity growth when firms move along the distance function changing their inputs levels over time."

14. With constant returns to scale, e_{nt} will equal 1, and hence the scale term in equation (3.6) will be equal to 0, as required.

Keep in mind also that the TFP index in equation (3.6) uses shadow prices, which are derived from the frontier, instead of market prices. If the regulator has access to input price data, it can also calculate the Törnqvist TFP change index. For the single output case this is

$$\ln(\text{TFP}_{n1}/\text{TFP}_{n0}) = (y_{n1} - y_{n0}) - 0.5 \sum_{k=1}^{K} [(s_{kn1} + s_{kn0}) \cdot (x_{kn1} - x_{kn0}), \qquad (3.9)$$

where s_{knt} is the cost share of the k-th input of the n-th firm in the t-th period.

Why should a regulator care about this calculation? Because any difference between the TFPC calculated from equations (3.6) and (3.9) must be due to allocative efficiency change (AEC). In fact, we can show that AEC is as follows: [15]

$$\text{AEC} = 0.5 \sum_{k=1}^{K} \{[(e_{kn1}/e_{n1} - s_{kn1}) + (e_{kn0}/e_{n0} - s_{kn0})] \cdot (x_{kn1} - x_{kn0})\}. \qquad (3.10)$$

This shows that the relative importance of distortions in the inputs mix can help explain TFP changes, and their relative importance may be a source of concern that the regulator may not be able to do much about. Indeed, allocative efficiency changes may result from distortions in factor markets not really under the control of the operator. Limited access to capital markets and national agreements with unions unrelated to the operator's specialized employment needs are two common examples of sources of allocative inefficiency for which the operator should not necessarily be blamed. Understanding that this is the case is a matter of fairness. Chapter 4 provides a detailed description of the application of these production frontier and Törnqvist methods to sample data.

---

15. This result will be exact when there is no noise in the model, that is, when we have a deterministic frontier. The expression in equation (3.10) has a nice intuitive interpretation. Essentially it shows that the TFPC index that we constructed in equation (3.6), is equivalent to a Törnqvist index that uses shadow prices instead of market prices to calculate the input share weights. These shadow shares are equal to the production elasticities deflated by the returns to scale elasticity. This deflation ensures that the shares sum to 1 as required. Thus the AEC measure in equation (3.10) will pick up the effects of any convergence or divergence in the differences between shadow prices and market prices, which may be due to regulatory and other change. If shadow prices equal market prices in both periods, this term will clearly be equal to 0. Furthermore, if shadow prices and market prices do not change between periods, the term will also be 0.

This quick introduction to the main concepts that regulators are likely to come across in the literature would not be complete without some brief comments on a few of the simplest, and yet common, hypothesis tests regulators will want to care about. Generally, testing for Cobb-Douglas versus translog is not a bad idea, as is testing for neutral versus non-neutral technical change in any model aimed at measuring efficiency in a regulated industry for which few data are available. If one of these sets of restrictions holds, fewer parameters have to be estimated and the statistical results can be more reliable with the same database size.

These types of tests are essentially based on likelihood ratio tests, which compare the likelihood function value of each model, for instance, does the translog model do a significantly better job of explaining variation in the sample data relative to the Cobb-Douglas function? They are quite routinely carried out in the literature to test these kinds of simple assumptions and are quite simple to implement. For instance, to test for neutral technical change in a production frontier with K inputs the steps are as follows:

1. Estimate the standard, unrestricted translog model and note the log-likelihood function (LLF) value of this unrestricted model (LLF_U).
2. Estimate the restricted model, where the K $x_i t$ variables, which would imply a non-neutral technical change, are omitted, and note the restricted LLF value (LLF_R).
3. Calculate the likelihood ratio test value, which is two times the difference between these two LLF values.
4. Reject the null hypothesis of neutral technical change if the test value exceeds the critical value, obtained from statistical tables. The likelihood ratio test statistic has a chi-square distribution, with degrees of freedom equal to the number of restrictions, in this case K.[16]

Cost Frontiers, Single Output Case

Cost frontiers are commonly used, simply because cost data seem to be much easier to come by. Ignoring the significant conceptual issues raised by cost functions in noncompetitive sectors, the main challenge for most

---

16. The procedure for the Cobb-Douglas versus translog test is similar. In this case the restricted model (the Cobb-Douglas) will only contain the first-order terms and the number of restrictions will be larger—$K(K + 1)/2$—if a time trend is included. Furthermore, looking at efficiency scores and ranks before and after imposing restrictions is always wise to see if the imposition of restrictions has a big effect.

regulators in developing countries without a strong tradition of good accounting standards is to make sure that the data mean something. The
data must be comparable and consistent over time, and the definitions of
the various cost concepts must be what most accountants would expect
them to be. This is not always easy to achieve in developing countries
where manipulating accounting data for tax reasons continues to be quite
widespread.

If and when these data are available, the most common functional form
found in the literature is a translog cost function, which essentially has cost
as a function of input prices and the production level. As for the production frontier, technical change is easy to incorporate, and this is often done
when long enough time series are available to track down this change. A
typical translog cost function estimated in the utilities or transport sector
takes the following form:

$$c_{nt} = \alpha_0 + \sum_{i=1}^{K} \alpha_i w_{int} + 0.5\sum_{i=1}^{K}\sum_{j=1}^{K} \alpha_{ij} w_{int} w_{jnt} + \beta_1 y_{nt} + 0.5\beta_{11} y_{nt}^2$$

$$+ \sum_{i=1}^{K} \gamma_i w_{int} y_{nt} + \sum_{i=1}^{K} \delta_i w_{int} t + \phi_1 y_{nt} t + \lambda_1 t + 0.5\lambda_{11} t^2 + v_{nt} + u_{nt},$$

(3.11)

where c_{nt} is the log of total cost, y_{nt} is the log of output quantity, w_{int} is the
log of i-th input price, t is a time trend that is included as a proxy for technical change, v_{nt} is a noise error term, u_{nt} is the cost inefficiency term, and
the Greek letters represent unknown parameters to be estimated. Cost inefficiency will contain the combined effects of technical and allocative efficiency. The subscripts n and t index firm and time period, respectively. The
error terms, v_{nt} and u_{nt}, are assumed to be distributed in the same way as in
the production frontier case, except that the u_{nt} term is added, not subtracted, because inefficiency in this context means higher costs, while in
the production frontier case it meant less output.

Note that in the literature homogeneity restrictions are typically imposed
on this function, that is,[17]

$$\sum_{i=1}^{K} \alpha_i = 1, \quad \sum_{i=1}^{K} \alpha_{ij} = 0 \ (j=1,2,\ldots,K), \quad \sum_{i=1}^{K} \gamma_i = 0, \quad \sum_{i=1}^{K} \delta_i = 0.$$ (3.12)

---

17. These restrictions ensure that the function is homogenous of degree one in
input prices. For example, this property ensures that a 10 percent increase in all
input prices will result in a 10 percent increase in costs.

These restrictions can easily be imposed by estimating a model where the cost and K-1 input prices are deflated by the K-th input price. The parameters associated with the K-th input can then be calculated using the estimated parameters and the restrictions defined in equation (3.12).[18]

The rest of the process mirrors that discussed for the production frontier. The TFPC for each firm between any two time periods is calculated using the estimates of the coefficients of the cost frontier. The general formula to calculate the log of the TFPC between periods $t = 0$ and $t = 1$ for the n-th firm is

$$\ln(\text{TFP}_{n1}/\text{TFP}_{n0}) = \ln(\text{CE}_{n0}/\text{CE}_{n1}) - 0.5\left[(\partial c_{n0}/\partial t) + (\partial c_{n1}/\partial t)\right]$$
$$+ 0.5\left[(1-\varepsilon_{n0}) + (1-\varepsilon_{n1})\right] \cdot (y_{n1} - y_{n0}), \tag{3.13}$$

where the three terms on the right-hand-side of equation (3.13) are the cost efficiency change (CEC), TC, and SEC terms, respectively.[19]

The cost efficiency measure, CE_{nt}, is the cost efficiency prediction of the n-th firm in the t-th time period and is calculated from the cost frontier estimated. This measure takes a value between 1 and infinity and is routinely reported by the FRONTIER computer program.[20]

---

18. Note that we have not used Shephard's Lemma to derive the first-order cost share equations, and we have not suggested estimating them jointly with the cost frontier. We have done this for many reasons. First, inclusion of the cost share equations makes estimation extremely complicated, and we are not confident that the possible gains in estimation efficiency warrant the extra effort. Second, the standard inclusion of the cost share equations implies that there is no systematic deviation from cost-minimizing behavior in this industry. This is unlikely in government-owned or regulated firms. One can specify a model where extra parameters are included to allow for systematic departure from allocative efficiency (see, for example, Balk 1998), but these shadow cost models are quite complicated to estimate, and one must then wonder if there will be any estimation efficiency gains.

19. This decomposition is based upon that presented in Kumbhakar and Lovell (2000), which was derived using total differential methods. However, we have converted their differential formula into an exact index number formula. This is done in the same way that Orea (2002) has done for the distance function case, which we used in our earlier production frontier discussion. The derivation involves the use of the translog identity.

20. This is equal to the conditional expectation of $\exp(u_{nt})$, given the value of $(v_{nt}+u_{nt})$. The FRONTIER computer program (Coelli, 1996b) reports the cost efficiency score as a value between 1 and infinity, with a value of 1 indicating cost efficiency. Most studies, however, report the inverse of this value, which will vary between 0 and 1, where a value of 1 indicates cost efficiency. Another computer

The TC measure is the mean of the technical change measures evaluated at the period 0 and period 1 data points with the cost frontier. This requires calculating the partial derivatives of cost with respect to time at each data point as follows:

$$\partial c_{n1}/\partial t = \lambda_1 + \lambda_{11}t + \sum_{k=1}^{K} \delta_k w_{knt} + \phi_1 y_{nt}. \tag{3.14}$$

The final term in equation (3.13), which measures the change in scale efficiency, requires calculation of the output elasticities

$$\varepsilon_{nt} = \partial c_{nt}/\partial y_{nt} = \beta_1 + \beta_{11} y_{nt} + \sum_{i=1}^{K} \gamma_i w_{int} + \phi_1 t \tag{3.15}$$

at each data point.[21]

Recall that in the production frontier case, when price information is available, the regulator can calculate an AEC component, which is equal to the difference between the TFPC measure obtained from the production frontier and a Törnqvist TFPC measure. This AEC measure was presented in equation (3.10). In a similar way, in the cost frontier case with information on input quantities, a Törnqvist TFPC index can be calculated and the difference between this index and the cost-based index is equal to

$$AEC = 0.5 \sum_{k=1}^{K} \{ [(\kappa_{kn1} - s_{kn1}) + (\kappa_{kn0} - s_{kn0})] \cdot (w_{kn1} - w_{kn0}) \}, \tag{3.16}$$

which will not be equal to 0 when the observed cost shares, s_{int}, differ from the "efficient" cost shares

$$\kappa_{knt} = \partial c_{nt}/\partial w_{knt} = \alpha_k + \sum_{i=1}^{K} \alpha_{ki} w_{int} + \gamma_k y_{nt} + \delta_k t. \tag{3.17}$$

---

program that performs DEA Malmquist indexes is OnFront, produced by the EMQ Group (http://www.emq.se/software.html).

21. This is equal to the inverse of the standard returns to scale elasticity. As before, when we have constant returns to scale this will equal 1, and thus the scale term in equation (3.13) will be equal to 0, as required.

Thus in this cost frontier case two terms in the TFP calculations involve changes in allocative efficiency, namely, the CEC, which also contains the effects of technical efficiency changes, and this AEC term.[22]

All this assumes that the estimated cost frontier actually reflects cost-minimizing behavior. If this is incorrect because of systematic deviations from allocative efficiency, for example, as a result of a regulatory bias such as rate of return regulation, then the link (or duality) between the cost frontier and the production frontier is lost, and thus our measures of allocative efficiency, technical efficiency, scale efficiency, and technical change will all be incorrect. This is one of the main reasons why some efficiency specialists are reluctant to rely on the cost frontier approach despite its widespread use among regulators (furthermore, Coelli and Cuesta 2000 and Mundlak 1996 indicate that dual estimators are often more inefficient than primal estimators). The main arguments for the use of the cost frontier are that it can accommodate multiple outputs, and also because in most cases the input prices are more likely to be exogenous than the input quantities. However, as we discuss next, the input distance function may provide an even better alternative.

Multiple Output Case

What happens when the regulated firm has outputs that are not homogenous enough to be integrated into a single output? Suburban passenger and long distance railways services, for instance, are not readily comparable, and neither are the water distribution service and the sewerage treatment business. Yet for many of the operators providing these multiple outputs, the inputs are shared and jointly determine the production process. How then can a regulator assess the efficiency of each business? Two

---

22. Any attempt to understand the meaning behind these two allocative efficiency components is likely to be frustrating. Consider some special cases instead. If the firm is allocatively efficient in both periods, then AEC is equal to 0 and CEC is due solely to a change in technical efficiency. Alternatively, assume there have been no price or output changes, but that the firm has changed the quantity of capital to labor, and hence has reduced the total cost of producing a particular output level. In this case the AEC term will be 0, but the total cost will fall, and thus cost efficiency will improve. Finally, assume that output and input quantities remain constant, but the relative price of capital to labor changes so that the total cost has fallen (this could be an accidental or anticipated allocative improvement). In this case the observed cost will fall, but what happens to the predicted minimum cost for this firm is hard to predict.

possible options are cost frontiers and an input distance function.[23] The first is the most common in the literature, and because it has been so common we discuss it despite our reluctance to deal with cost frontiers in regulated industries. The second option is a much more recent addition to the toolbox that provides a promising alternative for regulators.

Multiple Output Cost Frontier

Consider the situation of a regulator monitoring an operator producing M outputs with K inputs. As usual capital, labor, and "other" are standard inputs, but each one of these categories can be further disaggregated. A multiple output translog cost frontier is defined as

$$
\begin{aligned}
C_{nt} = \alpha_0 &+ \sum_{i=1}^{K} \alpha_i W_{int} + 0.5 \sum_{i=1}^{K} \sum_{j=1}^{K} \alpha_{ij} W_{int} W_{jnt} + \sum_{i=1}^{M} \beta_i y_{int} + 0.5 \sum_{i=1}^{M} \sum_{j=1}^{M} \beta_{ij} y_{int} y_{jnt} \\
&+ \sum_{i=1}^{K} \sum_{j=1}^{M} \gamma_{ij} W_{int} y_{jnt} + \sum_{i=1}^{K} \delta_i W_{int} t + \sum_{i=1}^{M} \phi_i y_{int} t + \lambda_1 t + 0.5 \lambda_{11} t^2 + v_{nt} + u_{nt},
\end{aligned}
\tag{3.18}
$$

where all notation is as previously defined.

As before, we need to place a restriction on this function to ensure the homogeneity of degree one in input prices of this function, which says that the multiplication of all input price by any constant value multiplies the costs by the same constant. The required homogeneity restrictions are

$$
\sum_{i=1}^{K} \alpha_i = 1, \quad \sum_{i=1}^{K} \alpha_{ij} = 0 \ (j = 1, 2, \ldots, K), \quad \sum_{i=1}^{K} \gamma_{ij} = 0 \ (j = 1, 2, \ldots, M), \quad \sum_{i=1}^{K} \delta_i = 0.
\tag{3.19}
$$

The TFP change for each firm between any two time periods can be calculated from the econometric estimates of the coefficients of this cost model. The log of the TFP change between period $t = 0$ and $t = 1$ for the n-th firm is equal to

$$
\begin{aligned}
\ln(TFP_{n1}/TFP_{n0}) = \ln(CE_{n0}/CE_{n1}) &- 0.5[(\partial c_{n0}/\partial t) + (\partial c_{n1}/\partial t)] \\
&+ 0.5 \sum_{i=1}^{M} [(SF_{n0} \varepsilon_{in0} + SF_{n0} \varepsilon_{in0}) \cdot (y_{in1} - y_{in0})]
\end{aligned}
\tag{3.20}
$$

---

23. We choose an input distance function instead of an output distance function because the input distance function is best suited to the case of endogenous inputs and exogenous outputs, which is a reasonable assumption in most network industries.

where the three terms on the right-hand-side of equation (3.20) are the CEC, TC, and SEC terms, respectively.[24] The cost efficiency measure, CE_{nt}, is the same as specified for the single output case. The technical change measure is the mean of the technical change measures evaluated at the period 0 and period 1 data points. For firm n in period t this is

$$\partial c_{nt} / \partial t = \lambda_1 + \lambda_{11} t + \sum_{i=1}^{K} \delta_i w_{int} + \sum_{i=1}^{M} \phi_i y_{int} . \tag{3.21}$$

The final term in equation (3.20), which measures the change in scale efficiency, requires calculation of the output elasticities

$$\varepsilon_{jnt} = \partial c_{nt} / \partial y_{jnt} = \beta_1 + \sum_{i=1}^{M} \beta_{ij} y_{int} + \sum_{i=1}^{K} \gamma_{ij} w_{int} + \phi_j t \tag{3.22}$$

for each output at each data point, and the calculation of the scale factors

$SF_{nt} = (\varepsilon_{nt} - 1) / \varepsilon_{nt}$ at each data point, where $\varepsilon_{nt} = \sum_{i=1}^{K} \varepsilon_{int}.$[25]

Once more, just as in the single output cost frontier case, with information on input quantities and output prices a Törnqvist TFPC index (see equation 3.6) can be calculated as

$$\ln (TFP_{n1} / TFP_{n0}) = 0.5 \sum_{j=1}^{M} \left[(r_{jn1} + r_{jn0}) \cdot (y_{jn1} - y_{jn0}) \right]$$
$$- 0.5 \sum_{i=1}^{K} \left[(s_{in1} + s_{in0}) \cdot (x_{in1} - x_{in0}) \right], \tag{3.23}$$

where r_{jnt} is the revenue share of the j-th output for the n-th firm in the t-th year. The difference between equation (3.23) and the cost-based TFP index (equation 3.20) is equal to the allocative inefficiency measure as follows:

---

24. This decomposition is based on that presented in Kumbhakar and Lovell (2000), which was derived using total differential methods. However, we have converted their differential formula into an index number formula, as we did in the single output cost frontier.

25. This is equal to the inverse of the standard returns to scale elasticity. Note that if we have constant returns to scale, this will equal 1, and hence the scale term in equation (3.20) will be equal to 0, as required.

$$\text{AEC} = 0.5 \sum_{i=1}^{K} \left\{ \left[(\kappa_{in1} - s_{in1}) + (\kappa_{in0} - s_{in0}) \right] \cdot (w_{in1} - w_{in0}) \right\}$$

$$+ 0.5 \sum_{j=1}^{M} \left\{ \left[(\pi_{jn1} - r_{jn1}) + (\pi_{jn0} - r_{jn0}) \right] \cdot (y_{jn1} - y_{jn0}) \right\}. \tag{3.24}$$

The interpretation of this measure is somewhat more complex, as it contains two parts. The first part is due to input mix allocative inefficiency. That is, when the observed cost shares, s_{int}, differ from the efficient cost shares

$$\kappa_{knt} = \partial c_{nt} / \partial w_{knt} = \alpha_k + \sum_{i=1}^{K} \alpha_{ki} w_{int} + \sum_{j=1}^{M} \gamma_{kj} y_{int} + \delta_k t . \tag{3.25}$$

The second part of equation (3.24) is due to output mix allocative inefficiency. That is, when the observed revenue shares, r_{int}, differ from the efficient revenue shares $\pi_{mnt} = \varepsilon_{mnt} / \varepsilon_{nt}$, that is, when shadow prices deviate from market (observed) prices.[26]

Input Distance Function

Increasingly, regulators are likely to come across input distance functions in the literature on efficiency measures in their sector (see Coelli and Perelman 1999, 2000 for applications to the railways sector and Carrington, Coelli, and Groom 2002 for an application to gas distribution). An input distance function can be thought of as a multiple output version of a production frontier. It considers the amount by which the input set of each firm may be proportionally contracted with the output set held fixed. This literature is somewhat more technical, but it is worth going through in some detail, as it is likely to become an important new instrument for analyzing efficiency in multi-output sectors.[27]

---

26. Most regulated firms face fixed input prices and fixed output quantities. Thus improvements in input mix allocative efficiency can be sought via adjustments to input quantities, while improvements in output mix allocative efficiency are sought through adjustments to the output prices, that is, tariff rebalancing.

27. Note that nonparametric input distance functions (input-oriented DEA models) have already been used in a number of regulatory analyses.

A translog input distance function with M outputs and K inputs may now be specified as

$$d_{nt} = \alpha_0 + \sum_{m=1}^{M} \beta_m y_{mnt} + \frac{1}{2} \sum_{m=1}^{M} \sum_{i=1}^{M} \beta_{mi} y_{mnt} y_{int} + \sum_{k=1}^{K} \beta_k x_{knt} + \frac{1}{2} \sum_{k=1}^{K} \sum_{j=1}^{K} \alpha_{kj} x_{knt} x_{jnt}$$
$$+ \sum_{k=1}^{K} \sum_{m=1}^{M} \gamma_{km} x_{knt} y_{mnt} + \sum_{i=1}^{K} \delta_i x_{int} t + \sum_{i=1}^{M} \phi_i y_{int} t + \lambda_1 t + 0.5 \lambda_{11} t^2, \tag{3.26}$$

where d_{nt} is the log of the input distance, y_{mnt} and x_{knt} are as defined before, and the Greek letters represent parameters to be estimated.

A necessary property of the input distance function is homogeneity (of degree +1) in inputs, which implies that

$$\sum_{k=1}^{K} \alpha_k = 1, \ \sum_{l=1}^{K} \alpha_{kl} = 0 \ (k = 1, 2, \ldots, K), \ \sum_{m=1}^{K} \gamma_{km} = 0 \ (k = 1, 2, \ldots, K), \ \sum_{k=1}^{K} \delta_k = 0. \tag{3.27}$$

Imposing these restrictions upon equation (3.26) yields the estimating form of the input distance function, in which the distance term, d_{nt}, can be viewed as an error term as follows,

$$-x_K = \alpha_0 + \sum_{m=1}^{M} \beta_m y_{mnt} + \frac{1}{2} \sum_{m=1}^{M} \sum_{i=1}^{M} \beta_{mi} y_{mnt} \ln y_{int} + \sum_{k=1}^{K-1} \alpha_k (x_{knt} - x_{Knt})$$
$$+ \frac{1}{2} \sum_{k=1}^{K-1} \sum_{j=1}^{K-1} \alpha_{kj} (x_{knt} - x_{Knt})(x_{jnt} - x_{Knt}) + \sum_{k=1}^{K-1} \sum_{m=1}^{M} \gamma_{km} (x_{knt} - x_{Knt}) y_{mnt}$$
$$+ \sum_{i=1}^{K-1} \delta_i (x_{int} - x_{Knt}) t + \sum_{i=1}^{M} \phi_i y_{int} t + \lambda_1 t + 0.5 \lambda_{11} t^2 - d_{nt}. \tag{3.28}$$

This error term explains the difference between the observed data points and those points predicted by the estimated transformation function. We can replace the distance term, $-d_{nt}$, with a composed error term, $v_{nt} - u_{nt}$, and estimate this function as we would do for a standard stochastic frontier function.

Now to measure TFPC relative to this estimated function we calculate[28]

---

28. Here we follow the general approach outlined in Orea (2002); however, we have adjusted the output distance function method in Orea (2002) to suit the input distance function used here.

$$\ln(\text{TFP}_{n1}/\text{TFP}_{n0}) = \ln(\text{TE}_{n1}/\text{TE}_{n0}) + 0.5\left[(\partial d_{n0}/\partial t) + (\partial d_{n1}/\partial t)\right]$$
$$+ 0.5\sum_{j=1}^{M}\left[(\text{SF}_{n0}\,\varepsilon_{jn0} + \text{SF}_{n1}\,\varepsilon_{jn1})\cdot(y_{jn1} - y_{jn0})\right], \qquad (3.29)$$

where the three terms on the right-hand-side of equation (3.29) are the TEC, TC, and SEC terms, respectively. Once more, the usual routine applies to the interpretations and measures of the three components of efficiency changes. The technical efficiency measure, TE_{nt}, is the technical efficiency prediction of the n-th firm in the t-th time period. It is the inverse of the input distance measure, and hence varies between 0 and 1 as required.[29] The technical change measure is the mean of the technical change measures evaluated at the period 0 and period 1 data points. For firm n in period t this is

$$\partial d_{nt}/\partial t = \lambda_1 + \lambda_{11}t + \sum_{k=1}^{K}\delta_k x_{knt} + \sum_{m=1}^{M}\phi_m y_{mnt}. \qquad (3.30)$$

The final term in equation (3.31), which measures the change in scale efficiency, requires calculation of the production elasticities

$$\varepsilon_{mnt} = \partial d_{nt}/\partial y_{mnt} = \beta_m + \sum_{i=1}^{M}\beta_{mi}y_{int} + \sum_{k=1}^{K}\gamma_{km}x_{knt} + \phi_m t \qquad (3.31)$$

for each output at each data point, and the calculation of the scale factors $\text{SF}_{nt} = (\varepsilon_{nt} + 1)/\varepsilon_{nt}$ at each data point, where $\varepsilon_{nt} = \sum_{m=1}^{M}\varepsilon_{mnt}$ is equal to the negative of the inverse of the standard returns to scale elasticity.[30]

With access to input price data, the Törnqvist TFPC index can also be calculated as in all the previous cases discussed so far. The difference between the Törnqvist TFPC index and the index in equation (3.29) will be due to allocative efficiency change as follows:

---

29. It is equal to the conditional expectation of $\exp(-u_{nt})$, given the value of $(v_{nt} - u_{nt})$. This value is routinely reported by the FRONTIER program; however, FRONTIER 4.1 does not explicitly include a distance function option. Nevertheless, you can estimate an input distance function by selecting the production function option, and entering the variables listed in equation (3.28).

30. Note that if we have constant returns to scale, ε_{nt} will equal −1, and hence the scale term in equation (3.29) will be equal to 0, as required.

$$
\begin{aligned}
\text{AEC} = 0.5 \sum_{m=1}^{M} & \left\{ \left[(r_{mn1} + \varepsilon_{mn1}/\varepsilon_{n1}) + (r_{mn0} + \varepsilon_{mn0}/\varepsilon_{n0}) \right] \cdot (y_{mn1} - y_{mn0}) \right\} \\
- 0.5 \sum_{k=1}^{K} & \left\{ \left[(s_{kn1} - e_{kn1}) + (s_{kn0} - e_{kn0}) \right] \cdot (x_{kn1} - x_{kn0}) \right\}.
\end{aligned}
\tag{3.32}
$$

Equation (3.32) has two components. The first measures output mix allocative efficiency effects. It will be nonzero if the market output shares, r_{mnt}, differ from the shadow output shares, $\varepsilon_{mnt}/\varepsilon_{nt}$, and if the output mix changes. Note that the shadow output shares will equal the output elasticities, ε_{mnt}, only under constant returns to scale, that is, when $\varepsilon_{nt} = -1$. The second component in equation (3.32) measures input mix allocative efficiency effects. It will be nonzero if the market input shares, s_{knt}, differ from the shadow input shares

$$
e_{knt} = \partial d_{nt}/\partial x_{knt} = \alpha_k + \sum_{i=1}^{K} \alpha_{ki} x_{int} + \sum_{m=1}^{M} \gamma_{km} y_{mnt} + \delta_k t ,
\tag{3.33}
$$

and if the input mix changes.

Some authors, such as Rodriguez-Alvarez 2000, argue that the econometric estimation of distance functions can be improved by the addition of cost share equations. For example, if you believed that cost minimization was a reasonable assumption (a questionable assumption in most network industries) and you had data on input cost shares, you could estimate the input distance function along with $K - 1$ input share equations, defined by equation (3.33), in a system of equations. However, no "canned" computer package allows this option, and you therefore have to do the programming from scratch. Alternatively, you could use the standard seemingly unrelated regressions method to estimate this system, which assumes all error terms are symmetric, and then adjust the intercept in the distance function using some type of corrected OLS method.[31]

---

31. Furthermore, you could test the cost-minimizing assumption by testing the hypothesis that the α_ks in the share equations equal the α_ks in the distance function. If this was rejected you could replace the α_ks in the share equations with different parameters, say η_ks. This would convert the system to a shadow cost-minimizing system, where nonzero values of $(\alpha_k - \eta_k)$ would reflect a difference between the shadow price and the market price for the k-th input. This is as done in Alvarez (2000). This appears to be a much cleaner way to deal with this issue than the shadow cost function approach suggested by Balk (1998) and others.

In many respects one could argue that the input distance function should be the function of choice in analyses of TFP in network industries. First, it avoids the problems associated with the cost function approach when cost minimization is violated. Second, it is much less complicated than the shadow cost function approach. Moreover, it permits having multiple outputs in a primal setting and avoids the endogenous regressors criticism that is sometimes leveled at the production frontier approach (see Coelli 2000 for more on this endogeneity issue).

However, having listed the advantages of the distance function approach, we hesitate to provide a strong recommendation for its use by the average regulator, given that it is such a new methodology. Perhaps it may be best for most regulators to wait a year or two before embracing distance functions. This will allow time for those regulators with access to high-level econometric expertise to put the method through its paces. Once this has been completed, we expect that input distance functions will become the method of choice in regulatory analyses.

In the meantime, you can avoid estimating a distance function by using PIN to aggregate outputs and then estimating an SFA production frontier. Alternatively, you could use PIN to aggregate inputs and then estimate an SFA input requirements frontier, that is, you regress an index of inputs against a vector of outputs. This latter strategy has the virtue of being consistent with the resource-conserving orientation of most utilities.

Malmquist DEA TFP Indexes

In this section we describe how a Malmquist TFP index can be constructed using input distance functions and how to estimate these input distance functions using DEA-like methods. Our methods are based on those outlined in Färe and others (1994), who used output distance functions. The input- and output-oriented approaches give identical TFP measures, but can provide slightly different scale efficiency decompositions. The input distance function is the natural one to use in regulated industries, where endogenous input quantities and exogenous output quantities are the norm.

The Malmquist TFP index measures the TFP change between two data points by calculating the ratio of the distances of each data point relative to a common technology. The Malmquist (input-oriented) TFP change index between period 0 (the base period) and period 1 (using period 1 technology as the reference technology) is given by

$$TFP_1 / TFP_0 = \frac{D_1(Y_0, X_0)}{D_1(Y_1, X_1)}, \tag{3.34}$$

where the notation $D_1(Y_0, X_0)$ represents the distance from the period 0 observation to the period 1 technology. A value of the ratio in equation (3.34) greater than 1 will indicate a TFP improvement, for example, a value of 1.04 corresponds to a 4 percent increase in TFP.[32]

An alternative Malmquist index can also be defined relative to the period 0 technology. Indeed, Färe and others (1994) defined their Malmquist TFP index as the geometric mean of these two indexes, that is, one evaluated with respect to period 1 technology and the second with respect to period 0 technology. Doing this yields

$$TFP_1 / TFP_0 = \left[\frac{D_1(Y_0, X_0)}{D_1(Y_1, X_1)} \frac{D_0(Y_0, X_0)}{D_0(Y_1, X_1)} \right]^{0.5}. \tag{3.35}$$

An equivalent way of writing this productivity index is

$$TFP_1 / TFP_0 = \frac{D_0(Y_0, X_0)}{D_1(Y_1, X_1)} \left[\frac{D_1(Y_0, X_0)}{D_0(Y_0, X_0)} \frac{D_1(Y_1, X_1)}{D_0(Y_1, X_1)} \right]^{0.5}, \tag{3.36}$$

where the ratio outside the square brackets measures the change in the input-oriented measure of technical efficiency between periods 0 and 1 (recall that the input distance measure is the inverse of the input-oriented technical efficiency measure).[33] The remaining part of the index in equation (3.36) is a measure of technical change. It is the geometric mean of the shift in technology between the two periods, evaluated at the period 0 data point and also at the period 1 data point.

---

32. Note that in this section we present our TFP indexes in ratio form instead of the log-change form used in the previous sections. This is because the translog functional form naturally lends itself to the calculation of TFP change in log-change form. When we make our empirical comparison in chapter 4 we will take the logarithms of our DEA results to make them comparable with our translog and Törnqvist results.

33. Farrell measures of efficiency correspond in each case to the expression or the reduction of the ray that passes through the origin (see Farrell 1957).

For most regulators of infrastructure services, however, the foregoing TFP index may not be a good option. Indeed, for the index in equation (3.36) to measure TFP change properly, CRS distance functions are required, otherwise the implicit weights will not add up to 1, and thus any scale efficiency gains (or losses) will be missed. Färe and others (1994) used CRS distance functions to calculate the index in equation (3.36). They also suggested a further decomposition of equation (3.36) whereby the CRS technical efficiency change measure could be decomposed into a "pure" technical efficiency change component and a scale efficiency change component. This is done by introducing some VRS distance functions to obtain

$$\text{TFP}_1 / \text{TFP}_0 = \frac{D_0^V(Y_0,X_0)}{D_1^V(Y_1,X_1)} \left[\frac{D_1^V(Y_1,X_1)}{D_0^V(Y_0,X_0)} \frac{D_0^C(Y_0,X_0)}{D_1^C(Y_1,X_1)} \right]$$

$$\times \left[\frac{D_1^C(Y_0,X_0)}{D_0^C(Y_0,X_0)} \frac{D_1^C(Y_1,X_1)}{D_0^C(Y_1,X_1)} \right]^{0.5}, \tag{3.37}$$

where the V and C superscripts refer to VRS and CRS technologies, respectively. Equation (3.37) thus gives a TEC measure, an SEC measure, and a TC measure, that is

$$\text{TFPC} = \text{TEC} \times \text{SEC} \times \text{TC}. \tag{3.38}$$

Some authors have criticized this decomposition because it measures technical change against the CRS technology instead of the VRS technology. Various alternatives have been proposed; however, none has yet gained widespread acceptance (see Balk 1999 and Grifell and Lovell 1999 for a discussion of this issue).

Färe and others (1994) showed that, given the availability of suitable panel data, we can calculate the required distances in equation (3.37) using DEA-like linear programs. These calculations are implemented in the computer program: data envelopment analysis program (DEAP) 2.1.[34] See chapter 7 in CRB for further details on the DEA programs involved.

Finally, note that Malmquist DEA TFP indexes use shadow prices, just like their parametric counterparts (translog production and distance functions) discussed earlier, and hence do not account for allocative efficiency

---

34. See Coelli (1996a) for more on the DEAP computer software. This software can be downloaded from http://www.uq.edu.au/economics/staff/coelli.htm.

changes. Calculating the Törnqvist index and interpreting any differences between the two measures as being primarily due to allocative efficiency effects is fine, but note that this allocative efficiency change measure will be a combination of input mix and output mix allocative efficiency. An advantage of the parametric decomposition methods is that you can obtain separate measures of these two components.[35]

Cross-Sectional TFP Comparisons

All the discussion in this chapter thus far has concentrated on the case where we wish to measure (and decompose) the TFPC for a firm between two time periods. Sometimes, however, the regulator needs to compare the TFP of a group of firms at one point in time. This is at the core of comparative performance evaluation for any regulator and is the key to effective yardstick competition. Consider a case where the regulator is monitoring N operators of quasi-competitive firms, typically local monopolies. This could be a group of regional ports or provincial water or electricity distribution companies. With N operators the regulator can construct $N(N-1)$ pairwise comparisons. The problem in that case is that standard Laspeyres, Paasche, Törnqvist, and Fisher indexes are nontransitive, that is, the pairwise comparisons will not necessarily give the same ranking of operators. For example, consider firms A, B, and C. We may calculate TFP indexes of $I(AB) = 1.1$ and $I(BC) = 1.1$ and $I(AC) = 1.15$, that is, A is 10 percent better than B, B is 10 percent better than C, and A is 15 percent better than C. These three indexes are not consistent, because we should have found that A was 21 percent better than C ($1.1 \times 1.1 = 1.21$).

Thus we need to "adjust" these inconsistent indexes to produce consistent indexes. The method most often used is the so-called EKS method, based on Elteto and Koves (1964) and Szulc (1964) (see chapter 4 in CRB). Caves, Christensen, and Diewert (1982a) showed that in the case of the Törnqvist index, there is a way to produce an adjusted Törnqvist index where

---

35. Creativity can help minimize the damage somewhat. If, for example, you have input prices but not output prices, say in a study of public hospitals, you could use the shadow revenue shares from the DEA (see Coelli and Rao 1999 for how to calculate these), along with the actual cost shares in the calculation of a Törnqvist index. The difference between this TFPC index and the Malmquist DEA TFP index should reveal information about the contribution of input-mix allocative efficiency.

a pair of firms is compared indirectly via the sample mean firm based on the EKS method. That is, by adjusting equation (3.4) we obtain

$$
\ln(\text{TFP}_{n1} / \text{TFP}_{n0})^{T(\text{EKS})} = 0.5 \sum_{j=1}^{M} \left[(r_{jn1} + \bar{r}_j) \cdot (y_{jn1} - \bar{y}_j) \right] - 0.5 \sum_{j=1}^{M} \left[(r_{jn0} + \bar{r}_j) \cdot (y_{jn0} - \bar{y}_j) \right]
$$
$$
- 0.5 \sum_{i=1}^{K} \left[(s_{in1} + \bar{s}_i) \cdot (x_{in1} - \bar{x}_i) \right] + 0.5 \sum_{i=1}^{K} \left[(s_{in0} + \bar{s}_i) \cdot (x_{in0} - \bar{x}_i) \right],
$$

(3.39)

where $\bar{r}_j$ is the j-th output share at the sample mean and $\bar{s}_j$ is the i-th input share at the sample mean. Note that when one observation is added or subtracted from the sample, we must recalculate all indexes in this case, because the sample means will change.

The decomposition of the TFP difference between two firms at one point in time (into TE, SE, and AE components) can be done in an identical way to that described for the time comparison, except that TC will not be an issue. However, in some cases the regulator may specify that it is only interested in TE comparisons across firms (it may perhaps believe that scale and AE are not controllable in the short run). In this case we need not bother with the between firm decomposition calculations, because the technical efficiency measures themselves will be sufficient.

What if Policy or Other Similar Variables Are Relevant?

Our examples so far do not include any environmental variables in the model, and yet these may be quite relevant. Changes in regulatory regimes, shocks such as the 1997 Asian financial crisis, weather patterns, or similar variables are often important here. The good news is that extending the method to include a term for environmental differences, either across firms or time, is easy. Indeed, we could view the time trend (technical change proxy) as a Z variable. If we do this we can see quite clearly how to calculate the effect of environment change, which we can label ZC. Instead of having partial derivatives with respect to time, we will have partial derivatives with respect to the Z variable(s), and so on.

Where do we include the Z variables? Do we put them in the translog function like a regular regressor variable or as part of the inefficiency error term in the SFA model as done in Battese and Coelli (1995)? The discussion of this option is beyond the scope of this book, but chapter 9 in CRB; Battese and Coelli (1995); and Coelli, Perelman, and Romano (1999) provide some discussion. The latter paper stresses that one must be careful when interpreting efficiency scores in the different models. The main point to remember is that if the Z variable is included in the translog function, the efficiency score obtained will be net of the effect of the Z variable, while if the Battese and Coelli (1995) model is used, one obtains gross efficiency scores, where the effect of the Z variable is included in the efficiency score.

Summing Up

Table 2.3 summarized the three main methods of performance measurement, including the main advantages and drawbacks of each approach, and emphasized the types of concerns a regulator should have. On the data side, for instance, assessing up-front the restrictions imposed on the methodology choice by the data is crucial. SFA and DEA are quite demanding in this respect. After a few years of operation, a regulator should have been able to generate enough information to be able to begin to use these methods in a detailed way. At the outset of their operations, however, most regulators will have to pick between using PIN or a restricted form of SFA or DEA, for example, impose constant returns to scale, use a simple functional form, aggregate inputs and outputs into only a few measures.

A look at the relative advantages of each method in table 2.3 shows that one advantage of SFA is that it is more amenable to modeling the effects of environmental variables than DEA. In the longer run, SFA methods are difficult to ignore, as demonstrated by the United Kingdom's experience, where they lie at the core of the policy debates between producers and regulators. The potential offered by these methods has to be balanced by their drawbacks, which in practice can be significant because they require not only good judgment, but also good econometric skills.

If the regulator chooses the SFA method, it must then choose between the cost frontier and production frontier approaches. These two functions can (and often do) provide differing results. The biggest differences will occur when there are large allocative distortions. This can be particularly important in regulated industries, where various factors such as the Averch and Johnson (1962) effect can introduce significant allocative distortions. When there are such allocative distortions, the estimates of the parameters of the cost frontier will be biased, and hence the various efficiency decompositions will also be biased.[36] Moreover, even if all firms are allocatively

---

36. This issue regarding the estimation of cost frontiers in the face of systematic allocative distortions is rather complex. Our concern primarily relates to the case when we wish to use the cost frontier estimates to decompose efficiency change

efficient, the directly estimated production frontier need not be identical to the production frontier implied by the estimated cost frontier. This is simply because a different object function is being maximized. Finally, note that allocative inefficiency need not only be the result of regulatory distortions, but can be due to various other factors, such as measurement errors, optimal long-run plans appearing to be suboptimal in the short run (typical in infrastructure industries), poor management decisions, or unexpected price changes or demand changes. The upshot of all this is that careful interpretation of results is always required. Furthermore, given the possible bias in cost frontier estimates in the presence of allocative inefficiency, one could argue that the production frontier approach is the preferred method for use in regulated industries. We discuss method choice in more detail later.

Finally, of the measurement methods discussed in this chapter, SFA and DEA have the advantage in that they allow a detailed decomposition of performance. The contribution of each factor to TFP—change in technology, technical efficiency, allocative efficiency, and scale efficiency—either at the firm level or the industry level, can be identified. They offer the regulator access to detailed information, which can help improve the quality of regulatory decisions.

---

into technical and allocative components. If we do not need to do this, then cost frontier estimation should be alright. That is, one can still estimate a cost frontier and measure the amount by which the firms become closer to or further away from the frontier to obtain cost efficiency change measures and measure the amount by which the cost frontier shifts over time to obtain a technical change measure (which should be a reasonable indicator of the shift in the production frontier if there has not been any systematic change in allocative efficiency during the sample period).

4

An Empirical Example

Consider a regulator that must monitor the performance of 20 railway companies. The regulator has annual data on the 20 railways over a five-year period. The data for this exercise have been randomly generated, but they provide the same kind of diversity that would be observed in the real world. Each firm uses three inputs, capital, labor, and other, to produce one output, measured in passenger kilometers.

The data, which are listed in table 4.1, have been generated as follows:

- Cobb-Douglas technology was used for data generation (a translog is used for estimation)
- Elasticities of capital, labor, and other are 0.40, 0.30, and 0.30, respectively, and hence the return to scale elasticity is 1.0
- Neutral technical change is 2 percent per year
- Technical efficiency change of approximately 1 percent occurs between years 2 and 3
- No scale efficiency change occurs
- No allocative efficiency change occurs
- No systematic (industrywide) allocative inefficiency is present, but a small amount of random allocative errors take place at the firm level.

We have used this data to measure TFP changes for each firm using

- Törnqvist PIN
- SFA production function
- SFA cost function
- SFA input distance function
- Malmquist DEA.

Table 4.1. *Railways Data*

		Quantities				Prices		
Firm	Year	Output	Capital	Labor	Other	Capital	Labor	Other
1	1	25.665	21.440	10.143	9.083	6.411	8.958	10.897
2	1	29.024	22.254	11.504	10.402	7.805	10.151	11.658
3	1	25.600	16.151	12.525	9.829	7.846	8.842	10.273
4	1	23.046	17.763	11.597	10.336	7.341	9.136	10.952
5	1	30.573	23.679	11.800	12.642	7.152	10.711	10.411
6	1	25.557	17.497	12.811	10.091	7.851	10.024	11.210
7	1	28.988	21.214	9.985	8.962	6.752	10.295	12.170
8	1	24.233	17.347	9.116	8.203	8.435	9.409	11.660
9	1	23.498	17.534	10.019	9.452	7.721	9.871	10.916
10	1	28.226	22.079	11.167	11.300	7.739	10.063	11.838
11	1	23.121	22.861	12.415	7.831	6.468	9.076	11.415
12	1	29.635	23.500	12.150	9.556	6.159	8.768	12.216
13	1	21.035	16.985	9.410	8.332	7.389	10.262	11.568
14	1	24.970	21.157	9.346	8.156	7.168	10.103	10.837
15	1	31.553	23.097	11.203	10.116	6.474	10.529	10.321
16	1	21.575	15.638	11.081	7.097	7.043	9.455	11.942
17	1	28.402	20.891	9.600	10.859	7.433	10.536	11.562
18	1	26.275	18.613	11.290	9.130	7.890	9.915	12.328
19	1	23.435	18.603	8.496	7.346	7.172	10.019	12.415
20	1	30.709	22.958	12.028	10.574	6.908	9.389	12.026
1	2	27.933	18.928	12.666	8.877	6.573	8.590	10.269
2	2	29.423	21.593	11.818	11.417	7.927	10.912	11.745
3	2	28.040	20.033	11.861	9.465	7.715	9.194	10.986
4	2	28.583	20.156	10.547	8.510	7.374	9.965	11.437
etc.								
16	5	23.141	14.194	9.673	8.108	7.022	9.545	11.609
17	5	31.264	16.767	11.515	10.514	7.549	10.374	10.789
18	5	24.785	16.614	12.143	9.875	8.039	9.917	12.063
19	5	25.980	21.780	8.589	8.046	7.293	10.892	12.666
20	5	30.742	24.233	10.510	8.829	6.389	10.267	11.977

All details on the estimation and calculation of our results are listed in a zip file, eg.zip, that can be found on the web site www.worldbank.org/wbi/regulation/efficiencybook. We calculated the results using both Excel and Shazam. In this chapter we will explain in some detail how the SFA production function results were obtained and then compare the results obtained using all five methods.

Estimation of an SFA Production Frontier

To use the FRONTIER computer program we need to construct a data file and an instruction file. Table 4.2 presents the data file required for the Frontier program. Recall that the model we wish to estimate is a translog stochastic production frontier, defined in equation (3.5) as

$$y_{nt} = \alpha_0 + \sum_{i=1}^{K} \alpha_i x_{int} + 0.5 \sum_{i=1}^{K} \sum_{j=1}^{K} \alpha_{ij} x_{int} x_{jnt} + \sum_{i=1}^{K} \delta_i x_{int} t + \lambda_1 t + 0.5 \lambda_{11} t^2$$
$$+ v_{nt} - u_{nt}, \quad n = 1, 2, \ldots, N, \ t = 1, 2, \ldots, T,$$

where all variables are as previously defined. In particular, recall that the y and x variables are logs of the original data.

In this example we have three inputs: capital, labor, and other, the logs of which we will label x_1, x_2, and x_3, respectively. Hence we have $K = 3$, $N = 20$, and $T = 5$. The Frontier program estimates a linear model, so if we want to estimate a translog model we need to supply transformed data to the program. Thus we need to construct a data file with the columns: firm number, period number, y, x_1, x_2, x_3, t, $x_1 x_1 / 2$, $x_1 x_2$, $x_1 x_3$, $x_1 t$, $x_2 x_2 / 2$, $x_2 x_3$, $x_2 t$, $x_3 x_3 / 2$, $x_3 t$, $tt/2$, where t is a time trend variable that takes the value 1, 2, 3, 4, or 5. Note that the cross-terms $(x_i x_j)$ are not multiplied by 0.5 because symmetry ensures that $x_i x_j = x_j x_i$.

The required columns of data are listed in table 4.2. Note that we have set all period numbers to 1 and set the firm numbers to vary from 1 to 100 (even though our data are derived from 20 firms over five years). We have done this to ensure that the Frontier program treats each observation individually. If we did not do this we would be imposing a restriction on the model that the technical efficiency of the i-th firm must be constant across all five years (which is imposed by the Frontier program when panel data are used). As we wish to measure technical efficiency change for each firm, we do not want to impose this restriction in this instance.[1]

Note also that the data in table 4.2 are all expressed in deviations from their sample means. This is simply a change in units of measurement and does not change the underlying data; however, it has the advantage that the estimated first-order parameters in the translog function can now be

---

1. Note that Frontier has a time-varying efficiency model option that could be used; however, this option restricts the technical efficiency of all firms to follow the same trend direction, that is, either all increasing over time or all decreasing over time, which is unlikely to be valid in many instances.

Table 4.2. Contents of Frontier Data File (pfn.dta)

Firm	Year	y	x1	x2	x3	x1x1/2	x1x2	x1x3	x1t	x2x2/2	x2x3	x2t	x3x3/2	x3t	tt/2
1	1	-0.05445	0.09343	-0.07618	-0.02310	0.00436	-0.00712	-0.00216	-0.18686	0.00290	0.00176	0.15236	0.00027	0.04621	2
2	1	0.06857	0.13070	0.04969	0.11245	0.00854	0.00649	0.01470	-0.26140	0.00123	0.00559	-0.09938	0.00632	-0.22490	2
3	1	-0.05695	-0.18988	0.13469	0.05575	0.01803	-0.02557	-0.01059	0.37976	0.00907	0.00751	-0.26937	0.00155	-0.11149	2
4	1	-0.16208	-0.09473	0.05777	0.10612	0.00449	-0.00547	-0.01005	0.18946	0.00167	0.00613	-0.11554	0.00563	-0.21223	2
5	1	0.12056	0.19277	0.07510	0.30744	0.01858	0.01448	0.05927	-0.38554	0.00282	0.02309	-0.15020	0.04726	-0.61489	2
6	1	-0.05863	-0.10980	0.15730	0.08210	0.00603	-0.01727	-0.00901	0.21961	0.01237	0.01291	-0.31460	0.00337	-0.16419	2
7	1	0.06731	0.08281	-0.09193	-0.03656	0.00343	-0.00761	-0.00303	-0.16562	0.00423	0.00336	0.18386	0.00067	0.07313	2
8	1	-0.11185	-0.11839	-0.18298	-0.12502	0.00701	0.02166	0.01480	0.23678	0.01674	0.02288	0.36595	0.00781	0.25003	2
9	1	-0.14264	-0.10771	-0.08852	0.01666	0.00580	0.00953	-0.00179	0.21542	0.00392	-0.00148	0.17703	0.00014	-0.03333	2
10	1	0.04067	0.12277	0.01994	0.19521	0.00754	0.00245	0.02397	-0.24555	0.00020	0.00389	-0.03987	0.01905	-0.39042	2
11	1	-0.15881	0.15760	0.12592	-0.17149	0.01242	0.01985	-0.02703	-0.31520	0.00793	-0.02160	-0.25185	0.01471	0.34299	2
12	1	0.08941	0.18515	0.10435	0.02760	0.01714	0.01932	0.00511	-0.37031	0.00544	0.00288	-0.20870	0.00038	-0.05520	2
13	1	-0.25337	-0.13949	-0.15124	-0.10947	0.00973	0.02110	0.01527	0.27899	0.01144	0.01656	0.30248	0.00599	0.21894	2
14	1	-0.08190	0.08015	-0.15801	-0.13079	0.00321	-0.01267	-0.01048	-0.16031	0.01248	0.02067	0.31602	0.00855	0.26159	2
15	1	0.15211	0.16786	0.02314	0.08459	0.01409	0.00388	0.01420	-0.33573	0.00027	0.00196	-0.04627	0.00358	-0.16917	2
16	1	-0.22801	-0.22214	0.01224	-0.26985	0.02467	-0.00272	0.05994	0.44429	0.00007	-0.00330	-0.02448	0.03641	0.53969	2
17	1	0.04691	0.06749	-0.13124	0.15548	0.00228	-0.00886	0.01049	-0.13498	0.00861	-0.02040	0.26248	0.01209	-0.31095	2
18	1	-0.03094	-0.04797	0.03090	-0.01800	0.00115	-0.00148	0.00086	0.09594	0.00048	-0.00056	-0.06180	0.00016	0.03601	2
19	1	-0.14533	-0.04851	-0.25343	-0.23546	0.00118	0.01229	0.01142	0.09701	0.03211	0.05967	0.50686	0.02772	0.47093	2
20	1	0.12499	0.16183	0.09426	0.12883	0.01310	0.01525	0.02085	-0.32367	0.00444	0.01214	-0.18851	0.00830	-0.25766	2
21	1	0.03024	-0.03121	0.14589	-0.04613	0.00049	-0.00455	0.00144	0.03121	0.01064	-0.00673	-0.14589	0.00106	0.04613	0.5
22	1	0.08220	0.10053	0.07658	0.20553	0.00505	0.00770	0.02066	-0.10053	0.00293	0.01574	-0.07658	0.02112	-0.20553	0.5
etc.															
98	1	-0.08932	-0.16157	0.10373	0.06048	0.01305	-0.01676	-0.00977	-0.32315	0.00538	0.00627	0.20746	0.00183	0.12096	2
99	1	-0.04225	0.10915	-0.24247	-0.14437	0.00596	-0.02647	-0.01576	0.21830	0.02940	0.03501	-0.48495	0.01042	-0.28875	2
100	1	0.12607	0.21586	-0.04068	-0.05154	0.02330	-0.00878	-0.01113	0.43172	0.00083	0.00210	-0.08136	0.00133	-0.10308	2

Note: Column headings do not appear in the data file, only data. Also note that the data in this table are presented to five decimal places. In the actual data file, all available decimal places appear.

58

Table 4.3. *Frontier Instruction File (pfn.ins)*

1	1 = ERROR COMPONENTS MODEL, 2 = TE EFFECTS MODEL
pfn.dta	DATA FILE NAME
pfn.out	OUTPUT FILE NAME
1	1 = PRODUCTION FUNCTION, 2 = COST FUNCTION
y	LOGGED DEPENDENT VARIABLE (Y/N)
100	NUMBER OF CROSS-SECTIONS
1	NUMBER OF TIME PERIODS
100	NUMBER OF OBSERVATIONS IN TOTAL
14	NUMBER OF REGRESSOR VARIABLES (Xs)
n	MU (Y/N) [OR DELTA0 (Y/N) IF USING TE EFFECTS MODEL]
n	ETA (Y/N) [OR NUMBER OF TE EFFECTS REGRESSORS (Zs)]
n	STARTING VALUES (Y/N)

Note: MU, DELTA0, and ETA are parameters not used in this case. They correspond to alternative model specifications estimated by FRONTIER.

directly interpreted as estimates of the production elasticities, evaluated at the sample means. For example, given that the geometric sample mean of x_1 is 19.528, the transformed data for capital (x_1) for the first observation is obtained as $\log(21.440) - \log(19.528) = 0.09343$.[2] Furthermore, note that the value of $x_1 x_1 / 2$ is calculated as $(0.09343)^2 / 2 = 0.00436$, and so on.

Table 4.3 shows the Frontier instruction file. Details on the use of the Frontier program are listed in the guide that accompanies the program. Some small points to note about this instruction file are that we have stated that there are 100 firms and 1 time period. We have done this to ensure that each observation is treated individually, as discussed earlier. Also note that we have specified that there are 14 regressors. This is the number of transformed regressors, not the original number of inputs (three).

Table 4.4 presents the Frontier output file. The final maximum likelihood estimates of the first-order parameters are 0.446, 0.310, 0.192, and 0.021, for capital, labor, other, and time, respectively. These are the estimated production elasticities (at the sample means), and are not too far away from the values we used to generate the data. Technical efficiency estimates for each firm and year appear at the bottom of the output file. Mean efficiency within the sample is equal to 0.932.

---

2. The time trend variable is also in deviations from the mean, that is, as the mean of the time trend variable is 3 in this instance, the mean-corrected trend variable is converted from (1, 2, 3, 4, 5) to (−2, −1, 0, 1, 2).

Table 4.4. *Frontier Output File Version 4.1c (pfn.out)*

instruction file = pfn.ins
data file = pfn.dta

Error Components Frontier (see Battese and Coelli 1992)
The model is a production function
The dependent variable is logged

the OLS estimates are:

	coefficient	standard-error	t-ratio
beta 0	0.33058179E+01	0.12440720E–01	0.26572561E+03
beta 1	0.43040305E+00	0.53572754E–01	0.80339916E+01
beta 2	0.19611089E+00	0.60628346E–01	0.32346403E+01
beta 3	0.31416264E+00	0.54687309E–01	0.57447082E+01
beta 4	0.22911311E–01	0.43633845E–02	0.52508118E+01
beta 5	0.27847879E+00	0.37853232E+00	0.73568035E+00
beta 6	–0.56806716E+00	0.54908081E+00	–0.10345784E+01
beta 7	–0.26579043E–01	0.67882473E+00	–0.39154500E–01
beta 8	–0.43432487E–01	0.35077743E-01	–0.12381779E+01
beta 9	0.10024329E+00	0.51697207E+00	0.19390465E+00
beta10	0.65179029E+00	0.54702372E+00	0.11915211E+01
beta11	0.64440160E–01	0.42965885E–01	0.14997983E+01
beta12	–0.43312441E+00	0.45616464E+00	–0.94949142E+00
beta13	–0.15728485E–01	0.37981186E–01	–0.41411252E+00
beta14	–0.64077692E–02	0.76858301E–02	–0.83371206E+00
sigma-squared	0.35150421E–02		

log likelihood function = 0.14876728E+03

the estimates after the grid search were:

beta 0	0.33651757E+01
beta 1	0.43040305E+00
beta 2	0.19611089E+00
beta 3	0.31416264E+00
beta 4	0.22911311E–01
beta 5	0.27847879E+00
beta 6	–0.56806716E+00
beta 7	–0.26579043E–01
beta 8	–0.43432487E–01
beta 9	0.10024329E+00

Table 4.4. *(continued)*

beta10	0.65179029E+00
beta11	0.64440160E–01
beta12	–0.43312441E+00
beta13	–0.15728485E–01
beta14	–0.64077692E–02
sigma-squared	0.65111363E–02
gamma	0.85000000E+00

mu is restricted to be zero
eta is restricted to be zero

[iterations ommitted]

the final mle estimates are:

	coefficient	standard-error	t-ratio
beta 0	0.33887447E+01	0.78940146E–02	0.42928026E+03
beta 1	0.44564014E+00	0.35290882E–01	0.12627628E+02
beta 2	0.30963504E+00	0.48691831E–01	0.63590758E+01
beta 3	0.19167522E+00	0.49830213E–01	0.38465662E+01
beta 4	0.21243612E–01	0.18865739E–02	0.11260419E+02
beta 5	0.11692042E+00	0.22718818E+00	0.51464129E+00
beta 6	–0.59611680E+00	0.54151481E+00	–0.11008319E+01
beta 7	–0.37893013E+00	0.36624844E+00	–0.10346259E+01
beta 8	–0.13145646E+00	0.18557452E–01	–0.70837560E+01
beta 9	0.25584915E+00	0.64313341E+00	0.39781660E+00
beta10	0.48941144E+00	0.56345658E+00	0.86858767E+00
beta11	0.78107521E–01	0.22831617E–01	0.34210244E+01
beta12	–0.50127988E+00	0.37041790E+00	–0.13532820E+01
beta13	0.23579210E–01	0.15780459E–01	0.14942030E+01
beta14	–0.11090394E–01	0.42507786E–02	–0.26090265E+01
sigma-squared	0.80567253E–02	0.96483087E–03	0.83504017E+01
gamma	0.99999999E+00	0.42936285E–05	0.23290324E+06

mu is restricted to be zero
eta is restricted to be zero

log likelihood function =   0.16391176E+03

LR test of the one-sided error =   0.30288941E+02
with number of restrictions = 1
[note that this statistic has a mixed chi-square distribution]

(Table continues on the following page.)

Table 4.4. *(continued)*

number of iterations =   32
(maximum number of iterations set at: 100)
number of cross-sections = 100
number of time periods = 1
total number of observations = 100
thus there are: 0 observations not in the panel

[covariance matrix ommitted]

technical efficiency estimates:

firm	eff.-est.
1	0.87083904E+00
2	0.93986611E+00
3	0.99413928E+00
4	0.86070370E+00
5	0.96549978E+00
6	0.93637393E+00
7	0.99390547E+00
8	0.99861213E+00
9	0.92573976E+00
10	0.92659782E+00
11	0.76368843E+00
12	0.92250505E+00
13	0.87644387E+00
14	0.86912320E+00
15	0.99977050E+00
16	0.99540980E+00
17	0.98816537E+00
18	0.97605540E+00
19	0.93330052E+00
20	0.96730311E+00
21	0.95739502E+00
22	0.93493151E+00
23	0.93654632E+00

etc.

| 99 | 0.93321667E+00 |
| 100 | 0.99340205E+00 |

mean efficiency = 0.93195415E+00

TFP Calculation and Decomposition

We will now illustrate how the various components of TFP change are calculated. The full results are presented in the Excel file (eg.xls) in eg.zip, specifically, in the Excel worksheet named SFA prodn fn TFP. Here we will show how to calculate these various measures for the first firm between the first two time periods.

From our SFA maximum likelihood estimates results in table 4.4 we observe that[3]

$$\alpha_0 = 3.389, \quad \alpha_1 = 0.446, \quad \alpha_2 = 0.310, \quad \alpha_3 = 0.192, \quad \lambda_1 = 0.021$$
$$\alpha_{11} = 0.117, \quad \alpha_{12} = -0.596, \quad \alpha_{13} = -0.379, \quad \delta_1 = -0.131, \quad \alpha_{22} = 0.256$$
$$\alpha_{23} = 0.489, \quad \delta_2 = 0.078, \quad \alpha_{33} = -0.501, \quad \delta_3 = 0.024, \quad \lambda_{11} = -0.011$$

From table 4.2, the transformed data for firm 1 are

Year	y	$x1$	$x2$	$x3$	t
1	−0.054	0.093	−0.076	−0.023	−2
2	0.030	−0.031	0.146	−0.046	−1

The technical efficiency scores for this firm are 0.871 and 0.957 for years 1 and 2, respectively, thus the TEC is

$$\text{TEC} = \log(0.957/0.871) \times 100 = 9.476.$$

This implies that technical efficiency improved by 9.5 percent for this firm between periods 1 and 2.

To calculate TC we need to evaluate the derivative with respect to time at each data point, defined by equation (3.7). For the case of three inputs this is

$$\partial y_{nt}/\partial t = \lambda_1 + \lambda_{11}t + \delta x_{1nt} + \delta_2 x_{2nt} + \delta_3 x_{3nt}.$$

For firm 1 in period 1 this is

$$0.021 - 0.011(-2) - 0.131(0.093) + 0.078(-0.076) + 0.024(-0.023) = 0.025$$

---

3. The order in which the regressor parameter estimates are reported in the Frontier program is determined by the order in which the variables are listed in the data file.

and for period 2 it is

$$0.021 - 0.011(-1) - 0.131(-0.031) + 0.078(0.146) + 0.024(-0.046) = 0.047.$$

Thus we calculate TC as the average of these two numbers:

$$TC = (0.025 + 0.047)/2 \times 100 = 3.570.$$

This implies that technical change was 3.6 percent between periods 1 and 2 for this firm.

The final term in equation (3.6), which measures the change in scale efficiency, requires calculation of the production elasticities for each input at each data point. For the case of three inputs the three elasticities are

$$e_{1nt} = \partial y_{nt}/\partial x_{1nt} = \alpha_1 + \alpha_{11}x_{1nt} + \alpha_{12}x_{2nt} + \alpha_{12}x_{3nt} + \delta_1 t$$
$$e_{2nt} = \partial y_{nt}/\partial x_{2nt} = \alpha_2 + \alpha_{21}x_{1nt} + \alpha_{22}x_{2nt} + \alpha_{22}x_{3nt} + \delta_2 t$$
$$e_{3nt} = \partial y_{nt}/\partial x_{3nt} = \alpha_3 + \alpha_{31}x_{1nt} + \alpha_{32}x_{2nt} + \alpha_{32}x_{3nt} + \delta_3 t.$$

For period 1 these are

$$e_{111} = 0.446 + 0.117(0.093) - 0.596(-0.076) - 0.379(-0.023) - 0.131(-2) = 0.774$$
$$e_{211} = 0.310 - 0.596(0.093) + 0.256(-0.076) + 0.489(-0.023) + 0.078(-2) = 0.067$$
$$e_{311} = 0.192 - 0.379(0.093) + 0.489(-0.076) - 0.501(-0.023) + 0.024(-2) = 0.083$$

and for period 2 they are

$$e_{112} = 0.446 + 0.117(-0.031) - 0.596(0.146) - 0.379(-0.046) - 0.131(-1) = 0.504$$
$$e_{212} = 0.310 - 0.596(-0.031) + 0.256(0.146) + 0.489(-0.046) + 0.078(-1) = 0.265$$
$$e_{312} = 0.192 - 0.379(-0.031) + 0.489(0.146) - 0.501(-0.046) + 0.024(-1) = 0.274.$$

Hence the scale elasticities in periods 1 and 2 are

$$e_{11} = 0.774 + 0.067 + 0.083 = 0.924$$

and

$$e_{12} = 0.504 + 0.265 + 0.274 = 1.043,$$

and the scale factors are

$$SF_{11} = (0.924 - 1)/0.924 = -0.082$$

and

$$SF_{12} = (1.043 - 1)/1.043 = 0.041.$$

We then use this information to calculate the scale efficiency change component from equation (3.6), namely:

$$SEC = 0.5 \sum_{k=1}^{K} [(SF_{n0}e_{kn0} + SF_{n1}e_{kn1}) \cdot (x_{kn1} - x_{kn0})].$$

When there are three inputs the SEC for firm 1 between periods 1 and 2 becomes

$$0.5[(SF_{11}e_{111} + SF_{12}e_{112}) \cdot (x_{112} - x_{111})$$
$$+ (SF_{11}e_{211} + SF_{12}e_{212}) \cdot (x_{212} - x_{211})$$
$$+ (SF_{11}e_{311} + SF_{12}e_{312}) \cdot (x_{312} - x_{311})].$$

Inserting the relevant numbers we obtain

$$0.5[(-0.082 \times 0.774 + 0.041 \times 0.504) \cdot (-0.031 - 0.093)$$
$$(-0.082 \times 0.067 + 0.041 \times 0.265) \cdot (0.146 + 0.076)$$
$$(-0.082 \times 0.083 + 0.041 \times 0.274) \cdot (-0.046 + 0.023)] \times 100 = 0.322.$$

This implies that scale improvements have made a contribution of 0.3 percent to TFP change.

When we add together our TEC, TC, and SEC measures we obtain a TFPC measure of

$$TFPC = 9.476 + 3.570 + 0.322 = 13.367,$$

that is, a TFP change of 13.4 percent for firm 1 between periods 1 and 2.

This TFP change index uses shadow prices instead of market prices. If we have access to input price data, which we do in this example, we can also calculate an additional AEC component, as defined in equation (3.10), as follows:

$$AEC = 0.5 \sum_{k=1}^{K} \{[(e_{kn1}/e_{n1} - s_{kn1}) + (e_{kn0}/e_{n0} - s_{kn0})] \cdot (x_{kn1} - x_{kn0})]\}.$$

When there are three inputs, the AEC for firm 1 between periods 1 and 2 is

$$0.5\{[(e_{112}/e_{12} - s_{112}) + (e_{111}/e_{11} - s_{111})] \cdot (x_{112} - x_{111})$$
$$+ [(e_{212}/e_{12} - s_{212}) + (e_{211}/e_{11} - s_{211})] \cdot (x_{212} - x_{211})$$
$$+ [(e_{312}/e_{12} - s_{312}) + (e_{311}/e_{11} - s_{311})] \cdot (x_{312} - x_{311})\}.$$

For this we need the cost shares in each period, which are calculated to be 0.420, 0.278, and 0.302 for capital, labor, and other, respectively, in

period 1, and 0.384, 0.334, and 0.281 in period 2. For example, $s_{111} = p_1q_1/$
$(p_1q_1 + p_2q_2 + p_3q_3) = 6.411 \times 21.440/(6.411 \times 21.440 + 8.958 \times 10.14 + 10.897$
$\times 9.083) = 0.420$. That is, for firm 1 in period 1 capital costs are 42 percent of
total costs.

Inserting the relevant numbers we obtain a AEC measure of

$$0.5\{[(0.504/1.043 - 0.384) + (0.774/0.924 - 0.420)]\cdot(-0.031 - 0.093)$$
$$+ [(0.265/1.043 - 0.334) + (0.067/0.924 - 0.278)]\cdot(0.146 + 0.076)$$
$$+ [(0.274/1.043 - 0.281) + (0.083/0.924 - 0.302)]\cdot(-0.046 + 0.023)\} \times 100 = -6.139.$$

This implies that allocative efficiency made a negative contribution of
6.139 percent to TFP change. When this is added to our earlier TFPC measure we obtain a revised TFPC measure of 7.228 percent between period 1
and period 2.

In table 4.5, the first line contains all the results detailed before and corresponding to firm 1 and TFP changes between periods 1 and 2. Two TFP
change columns are presented in table 4.5. The first measure (TFPC1) does
not include AEC while the second measure (TFPC2) does include AEC. As
you can see, firms in our example exhibit great variability in TFPC. Positive and negative changes in TEC and AEC contribute the most significantly to TFPC. SEC is relatively low and TC is generally positive. Both
results seem to reflect the true values, 0 and 2 percent, respectively, we
choose for the design of the data.

We proceed in a similar way for each of the five alternative methods.
A full presentation of the calculations and results corresponding to these
methods are included in the eg.zip file. Box 4.1 lists the contents of this
zip file.

Comparison of Methods

Table 4.6 presents some summary information. It lists the averages of the
various TFP measures obtained using the five different methods and their
decompositions. These figures are the sample means of the 80 pair-wise
firm-level changes. Generally we observe that all methods have done a
reasonable job of measuring TFP change in this case. The TFPC2 measures
from the SFA approaches differ slightly from the PIN measure because of
the effects of noise.

All five methods do a reasonable job of measuring and decomposing
TFP change. The primal SFA methods (production and distance function)
tend to do marginally better than the other methods.

Table 4.5. *Production Function TFP Measures and Decomposition*

Firm	Year	TEC	TC	SEC	TFPC1	AEC	TFPC2
1	2	9.476	3.570	0.322	13.367	−6.139	7.228
2	2	−0.526	3.136	0.085	2.694	−2.949	−0.255
3	2	−5.968	5.795	0.513	0.340	3.280	3.620
4	2	14.609	4.304	0.025	18.938	6.250	25.187
5	2	2.722	3.557	0.990	7.270	0.602	7.872
6	2	−2.686	5.672	−0.217	2.770	2.611	5.381
7	2	−7.471	1.860	−2.100	−7.711	−1.017	−8.728
8	2	−2.174	3.540	0.571	1.936	0.523	2.460
9	2	−9.402	4.183	0.307	−4.911	2.471	−2.440
10	2	1.308	2.197	−0.423	3.082	−2.171	0.911
11	2	7.296	3.386	−0.201	10.481	−3.436	7.045
12	2	−3.414	1.354	−2.253	−4.313	4.862	0.549
13	2	8.588	4.694	−0.988	12.295	−2.017	10.278
14	2	−3.481	2.589	−0.099	−0.991	−7.711	−8.701
15	2	−6.002	2.815	−0.198	−3.386	−3.211	−6.597
16	2	−8.982	5.286	1.342	−2.354	2.971	0.618
17	2	−5.013	2.842	0.045	−2.126	−0.200	−2.326
18	2	−14.817	4.223	0.073	−10.520	1.603	−8.918
19	2	−0.312	2.667	−0.335	2.019	−5.716	−3.697
20	2	2.342	3.193	1.761	7.296	−3.148	4.148
1	3	−5.293	3.321	0.016	−1.955	0.815	−1.140
2	3	4.498	3.400	0.118	8.015	0.154	8.170
3	3	3.421	3.525	0.079	7.025	−1.441	5.585
etc.							
18	5	−7.498	2.739	0.047	−4.711	2.690	−2.021
19	5	−0.162	−0.409	−0.756	−1.327	0.216	−1.111
20	5	4.265	−1.919	−1.677	0.669	−0.180	0.489
mean		0.052	2.163	−0.002	2.214	−0.133	2.081

Note: TFP1 = TEC + TC + SEC, while TFPC2 = TFPC1 + AEC.

We need to note a few points. The SFA cost function approach has underestimated technical change; however, the underestimation of primal technical change by the dual cost function technical change measure is not unexpected. This is due to the presence of increasing returns to scale in the estimated cost function. For example, see equation 8.3.4 in Kumbhakar and Lovell (2000), which observes that the negative of the technical change measure from the cost function $(\partial c / \partial t)$ will be equal to the technical change

Box 4.1. *Description of Files in eg.zip*

Data generation	eggen.sha	Shazam code
	eggen.out	Shazam output
	eggen.dta	data generated for the example (table 4.1)
SFA production frontier	pfnmle.sha	Shazam code for Frontier data preparation
	pfnmle.out	Shazam output
	pfn.dta	Frontier transformed data (table 4.2)
	pfn.ins	Frontier instructions file (table 4.3)
	pfn.out	Frontier output file (table 4.4)
	pfn.txt	parameters and efficiency scores
SFA cost frontier	cfnmle.sha	Shazam code for Frontier data preparation
	cfnmle.out	Shazam output
	cfn.data	Frontier transformed data
	cfn.ins	Frontier instructions file
	cfn.out	Frontier output file
	cfn.txt	parameters and efficiency scores
SFA distance function	dfnmle.sha	Shazam code for Frontier data preparation
	dfnmle.out	Shazam output
	dfn.dta	Frontier transformed data
	dfn.ins	Frontier instructions file
	dfn.out	Frontier output file
	dfn.txt	parameters and efficiency scores
DEA—Malmquist	dea.dta	DEAP data file
	dea.ins	DEAP instructions file
	dea.out	DEAP output file
TFP calculations	eg.xls	Excel file containing several worksheets:
	Data	Data file (eggen.data) and PIN calculation
	SFA prodn fn data	SFA production frontier (pfn.dta)
	SFA prodn fn output	*idem* (pfn.out)
	SFA prodn fn TFP	*idem* (table 4.5)
	SFA cost fn data	SFA cost frontier (cfn.dta)
	SFA cost fn output	*idem* (cfn.out)
	SFA cost fn TFP	*idem*
	SFA distance fn data	SFA distance function (dfn.dta)
	SFA distance fn output	*idem* (dfn.out)
	SFA distance fn TFP	*idem*
	Malmquist DEA data	data file (dea.dta) for DEAP
	TFP malm	DEAP output (dea.out)
	TFP comparison	Average TFP change (table 4.6)
	Price-cap example	TE and TFP change (table 4.7)

Table 4.6. *Summary of Results*

Method	TEC	TC	SEC	TFPC1	AEC	TFPC2
Production function	0.052	2.163	−0.002	2.214	−0.133	2.081
Cost function	−0.102	1.846	0.376	2.119	−0.086	2.033
Distance function	0.054	1.880	0.216	2.150	−0.049	2.101
DEA	0.300	2.200	−0.300	2.100		
PIN						2.117
True	0.250	2.000	0.000	2.250	0.000	2.250

Note: TEC is cost efficiency change for the cost function case.
TFPC1 = TEC + TC + SEC, while TFPC2 = TFPC1 + AEC.

measure from the production function ($\partial y / \partial t$) multiplied by the cost function scale elasticity ($\partial c / \partial y$). That is, $-(\partial c / \partial t) = (\partial y / \partial t) \times (\partial c / \partial y)$. From our results we note that $\partial c / \partial y$ is 0.78 at the sample means. This explains why our dual measure of technical change is lower than the primal value.[4] Note also that if our estimated cost function had decreasing returns to scale, the dual measure would be larger than the primal measure, and under constant returns to scale the two measures will be equal.[5]

The cost function approach has also identified SEC when none was introduced in the data generation process. See equation 8.3.5 in Kumbhakar and Lovell (2000) for an explanation of why the primal and dual SEC measures will differ when one has nonconstant returns to scale. They show that the dual SEC measure will differ from the primal SEC measure by an additive factor of $(1 - e^{-1}) \times (\partial y / \partial t)$, where e is the primal scale elasticity.

The underestimation of technical change and overestimation of scale efficiency change is also evident in the input distance function, but to a lesser extent. The overestimation occurs because the input distance function is input oriented like the cost function; however, the differences are not as great in the distance function results because estimated scale elasticity in the distance function (1.19) is less than the cost function estimate (1.28).

---

4. This effect is not helped by the fact that our cost function estimates produce a mean scale elasticity estimate of 1.28 when the true value is 1.0; however, our production function estimate is much closer at 0.95.

5. This is true if the underlying production parameters are identical, but the production function parameters obtained from a directly estimated production function will rarely be equal to the parameters of the production function implied by an estimated cost function.

Overall, in this empirical exercise we have observed that the primal (production and distance function) SFA methods have done marginally better that the dual (cost function) SFA approach. However, note that this is only one example. Some kind of Monte Carlo simulation experiment could shed further light on the generality of these results. However, we stress that in this example we have generated the data assuming no systematic departure from allocative efficiency. If we had introduced an allocative distortion, as one would expect in most regulated and/or government owned industries, our dual approach would most likely have produced even poorer results.[6]

A Price Cap Regulation Example

Let us assume that the regulator of this railways sector has studied the foregoing results and has concluded that the production frontier results are preferable. We will now use these empirical results to illustrate how the regulator could use such information in setting price caps for these 20 firms over the coming five-year period.

In table 4.7 we present some detailed results (firm by firm and year by year averages) concerning TFPC and its decomposition. We observe that the annual average TFP growth rate for the whole sector over the period was equal to 2.081 percent, and that this was essentially due to TC of 2.163 percent. Consequently, we observe that the contribution of TEC, SEC, and AEC in this empirical example is relatively low. Thus the regulator could conclude that asking all firms to achieve a minimum 2 percent TFP growth per year over the coming five-year period would be reasonable.

Furthermore, it is evident from the final column of table 4.7 that some firms are inefficient relative to other firms in the sample. The levels of TE in the final year of the sample period (t = 5) vary considerably among the 20 firms from 1.000 for firm 14 (which is on the frontier) to 0.777 for firm 18. Thus the regulator may choose to ask those firms with TE less than 1 not only to achieve a rate of TFP growth equal to 2 percent per year, but also to achieve a degree of catch-up to the frontier.

---

6. Estimates of the translog functional form can sometimes suffer from violations of the regularity conditions set down in microeconomic theory. We tested monotonicity and convexity conditions in all our estimated functions and results of these tests are reported in the eg.xls file. The results indicate some violations at some data points. For more on this issue see Ryan and Wales (2000).

Table 4.7. *TE and TFPC Decomposition by Firm and Period*

Firm	TEC	TC	SEC	TFPC1	AEC	TFPC2	TE (t = 5)
1	0.602	2.209	0.182	2.993	0.951	3.943	0.973
2	−0.211	2.201	−0.036	1.955	0.076	2.031	0.984
3	0.999	2.294	−0.043	3.250	−0.192	3.058	0.951
4	1.228	2.188	−0.006	3.410	−0.013	3.397	0.881
5	0.106	1.765	0.261	2.132	0.146	2.278	0.999
6	−1.313	2.380	−0.184	0.883	−0.387	0.496	0.847
7	−0.305	1.711	0.139	1.546	−0.366	1.180	0.984
8	−1.508	2.179	0.235	0.906	−0.325	0.580	0.937
9	−1.138	1.931	−0.046	0.748	0.104	0.852	0.915
10	−0.473	2.005	−0.138	1.394	−0.180	1.214	0.928
11	1.360	2.123	−0.415	3.067	0.260	3.327	0.904
12	−0.143	2.170	−0.097	1.930	0.345	2.274	0.954
13	3.199	2.099	0.905	6.204	−0.753	5.451	0.915
14	0.761	1.695	0.556	3.012	−0.479	2.533	1.000
15	−0.860	1.497	0.261	0.898	−0.566	0.332	0.954
16	−0.750	2.157	−0.024	1.383	0.591	1.974	0.911
17	0.491	1.735	−0.065	2.161	1.130	3.291	0.998
18	−2.252	2.366	−0.185	−0.071	−0.081	−0.152	0.777
19	0.146	1.668	−0.260	1.554	1.299	2.853	0.933
20	−0.467	1.705	−0.367	0.872	−0.329	0.543	0.993
Year							
1	—	—	—	—	—	—	0.936
2	0.115	2.398	−0.099	2.414	0.119	2.533	0.937
3	0.384	2.158	0.345	2.887	−0.398	2.489	0.940
4	0.380	1.876	−0.288	1.968	0.218	2.187	0.943
5	−0.984	1.583	0.176	0.775	0.307	1.082	0.935
mean	0.052	2.163	−0.002	2.214	−0.133	2.081	0.938

— Not available.

Note: TFPC1 = TEC + TC + SEC, while TFPC2 = TFPC1 + AEC.

The regulator could set the firm-specific X-factors so as to ensure that each firm has a TE score of 1 by the end of the five-year period; however, this would require significant faith in the quality of the econometric estimates. A more conservative approach could be to ask those firms that are technically inefficient to reduce one-half of the inefficiency gap. For example, consider the case of firm 18, which has a TE score of 0.777 and is the most inefficient firm in the sample. The regulator could ask it to achieve the base level of 2 percent TFP growth per year, plus an additional $(1 - 0.777)/2 = 0.1115$, or 11 percent, catch-up over the five-year period, that is, 2.14 percent catch-up per year.[7] Thus the total X-factor for firm 18 would be $2 + 2.14 = 4.14$ percent per year.

We have performed similar calculations for each firm in the sample and present the results in table 4.8. Note, for example, that firm 14 is fully efficient, and hence it is given an X-factor of 2 percent because no catch-up is required for that firm. Overall we obtain an average catch-up factor of 0.62 percent, and thus an average X-factor of 2.62 percent.

A regulator should never use these performance measures in an entirely prescriptive manner. The X-factors proposed in table 4.8 should only be used as a basis for the regulator and the firm to begin discussions and negotiations. Each firm should be given the opportunity to explain to the regulator why it is "different." The firm needs to make a strong case to argue that the model has not captured an important factor that is relevant to its situation. For example, if one railway company covers a much more mountainous region than other firms in the sample, it could argue that its fuel expenses are higher.

This empirical example has not been an ideal illustration of the possible benefits of these methods. This is because we found that TEC, SEC, and AEC made negligible contributions to TFP growth, and hence the TFPC index was a good measure of TC (frontier shift). However, if we had found that some of the TFPC was due to these other factors, we could have adjusted our X-factors accordingly.

Why have we used the industry TFPC measure to set the X-factors instead of using the firm-specific TFPC measures reported in table 4.7? The individual TFPC values in table 4.7 vary quite a bit between firms. The TFPC2 measures range from 5.45 percent per year for firm 13 to a decline of 0.15 percent per year for firm 18. Perhaps these firm-level TFPC measures are a better indication of the potential TFP growth of these firms? Perhaps they reflect differences in operating environments, which we have not accounted for? Or perhaps they reflect differences in managerial motivation and/or ability?

Knowing which of these factors is more important is difficult. The regulator will need to consider each firm on a case by case basis, but should avoid the use of firm-specific TFPC measures at all costs, because the incentives in the price cap system will be lost. If firm 13 is told that it must

---

7. This is calculated by noting that $(1.1115)^{1/5} = 1.0214$.

Table 4.8. *Calculation of X-Factors*

Firm	TE	Catch-up	Frontier shift	X-factor
1	0.973	0.27	2	2.27
2	0.984	0.16	2	2.16
3	0.951	0.49	2	2.49
4	0.881	1.16	2	3.16
5	0.999	0.01	2	2.01
6	0.847	1.49	2	3.49
7	0.984	0.16	2	2.16
8	0.937	0.62	2	2.62
9	0.915	0.84	2	2.84
10	0.928	0.71	2	2.71
11	0.904	0.94	2	2.94
12	0.954	0.46	2	2.46
13	0.915	0.84	2	2.84
14	1.000	0.00	2	2.00
15	0.954	0.46	2	2.46
16	0.911	0.87	2	2.87
17	0.998	0.02	2	2.02
18	0.777	2.14	2	4.14
19	0.933	0.66	2	2.66
20	0.993	0.07	2	2.07
mean	0.938	0.62	2	2.62

achieve the highest X-factor because it achieved the best TFP growth over the past five years, it will quickly decide that seeking future TFP growth is not in its best interest.

Note, however, that a regulator may have reasons not to ask for the same level of technical change (frontier shift) from all firms in the sample. For example, if some railways are located in areas where population growth is slower, these railways may be less able to benefit from the productivity-enhancing technologies embedded in new capital, because their rates of capital investment are slower. If the regulator suspected that this was the case, it could conduct some additional empirical analysis where the firm-level TFPC measures are regressed against growth rates to see if there is a significant association between these factors. If a significant association is found, the regulator could use this information to adjust the X-factors.[8]

---

8. Rossi and Ruzzier (2000) provide a useful complement to the discussion in this chapter with a discussion of statistical tests that can be used to check consistency across methods.

5

Performance Measurement Issues in Regulation

In the previous three chapters we assumed that the regulator had access to good quality data. This assumption allowed us to describe the various concepts and methods without the distraction of the many complexities of the real world. In the remainder of this book we begin to relax this assumption and discuss some of the many practical problems that regulators often face.

In this chapter we discuss some of the issues that a regulator would need to think about when attempting to use performance measures. Consider a standard problem a regulator will face. Say a new regulator must monitor the performance of an electricity distribution company, a sanitation company, a railway company, or a port. In some cases it may have a large number of in-country comparators available, but in some other cases the regulator may have to rely on an international comparison. This section tries to spell out the sequence of stages a regulator must go through before it can announce its estimate of the X that will apply to the firm it is supposed to monitor.

The first stage is to figure out what the regulator wants to do. Its main goal is to get the firm it is supposed to monitor to produce at minimum cost, given the exogenous (and perhaps changing) environment it faces. The regulator will also look at various financial ratios as well as a safeguard. In cases when it monitors several firms, the regulator may believe that some of the firms are more inefficient than others, and may therefore consider setting differential price caps in the first regulatory period, with a view to stimulating convergence toward the most efficient performance possible by the end of the five-year period.

Setting a Single X-Factor for All Firms

Assume that the regulator has access to some industry-level data and has constructed a rough measure of industry TFP change for the last five years using PIN methods. What are some of the potential pitfalls in setting the X-factor equal to this TFP measure?

- One could argue that with this approach, the consumer received all the benefits of TFP growth, while the producers only earn normal profits. Perhaps we should set a lower rate per year so that the firms make some extra dollars? But then at the end of five years these firms will be earning a large extra profit per year. Do we take it all away at the next cap setting? Or would we again be sending the wrong message to the operators?
- This rate may be too low if the monitored firms are inefficient relative to other firms in other countries. For example, we could look at the United Kingdom, where most of these rates have been calculated at least once before. If our TFP rate is lower, the difference may be an indication of what can be achieved when regulation is tightened and accumulated fat is cut from firms, especially in the early years of the new regulatory regime. Furthermore, international comparisons of TFP levels across different countries may also provide some indication of the relative productivity of the local industry.
- Much past and future TFP growth could be driven by improvements embedded in new capital. If the industry is overcapitalized (excess capacity) at present, the new regulatory environment may slow new investment. This may lead to lower TFP growth derived from embodied technical change. This may be the case in rail or ports, where excess investment has been the norm in many developing countries; however, in most developing countries the concern tends to be undercapitalization rather than overcapitalization.
- Investment may also be slow if demand growth is slow. New environmental laws may retard output growth in the next five years relative to the previous period. This may also affect the average level of energy sold per customer, which could again influence the rate of TFP growth.
- The position in the business cycle is important. If the next five years are part of the down cycle we might see an effect on demand growth that will flow through to TFP growth, so perhaps we should set a lower X factor.

We have listed five examples here. There are a number of additional ones that have not been discussed. The key issue is to not use your performance measures in a vacuum. Always be on the look out for reasons why a model that is applied to past data may not be directly applicable to the future.

For now, let us assume that we have considered all these issues and in 2001 have set the industry X-factor at 2 percent per year. Now what happens if in 2005 we find that the industry has actually achieved 3 percent per year? Do we immediately remove the extra 5 percent (1 percent per year) the firms have built up and slap a new X-factor of 3 percent on them for the 2006–10 period? This prospect may entice firms to play a game—such as using extra inputs in the final year of the five-year price cap period so as to depress the measured TFP growth—which is not the incentive we want to introduce. Rather than remove the 5 percent immediately, we could take it back gradually, say by adding a 1 percent "claw-back factor" to our base X-factor over the next five years. This means the industry can benefit from beating the price cap for a longer period of time, but eventually it must return to normal profit levels as would occur in a competitive industry. These are the types of judgment calls regulators must regularly make.[1]

Setting Firm-Specific X-Factors

The job is not over yet, because each of the firms will argue for special treatment. In particular, the least efficient firms are likely to try to convince the regulator that they have good reasons for being less efficient. This means that the regulator should be able to assess the relative efficiency of each one of the firms. This suggests two important questions, namely:

- What should be used to measure TFP differences between firms?
- Once these measures have been calculated, how should they be used in setting price caps?

Method choice depends partly on what data we have available and partly on what we wish to do with the results. Assume that we have reasonable data, for example, two to four years of data for each firm. It can then estimate TFP for each firm using transitive PIN methods. The question then is,

---

1. One problem with this option is that it may still discourage firms from innovating in the latter years of the five-year price cap period. One way in which one can try to avoid this is to allow the firms to keep any supernormal profits for five years from the year that they first earn them.

are there any components of TFP that we may wish to exclude, for example, the effects of differences in output characteristics and environment, of scale economies, or of allocative inefficiency? If we are interested in scale or allocative efficiency, we need to use a frontier method such as DEA or SFA to do this.

Which frontier method should we use? Here the opinions of various efficiency measurement specialists tend to differ. We would argue that DEA may not be the best method to use for a number of reasons. First, DEA does not account for possible noise and/or other interfering factors, which are likely to be quite important in reforming or adjusting economies or sectors. Second, one must decide ahead of time the sign of the effect of each Z variable (environmental variable) upon efficiency so that we know if it is to be included as an input or as an output, as discussed in the next section. Third, one cannot determine the significance of the effect of the Z variables. Fourth, the shadow prices in DEA can vary a good deal across the sample, with some zero prices often found for some firms in the sample, which are difficult to justify (see CRB for further discussion of the relative merits of DEA and SFA methods).

SFA is arguably a better method, but it also has potential problems, in particular, the standard SFA method uses specific assumptions on residual skewness to separate inefficiency from measurement errors, which some econometricians criticize. One alternative is to use OLS to estimate the SFA model and then use expert judgment to adjust the intercept parameter.[2] However, such "expert judgment" may be susceptible to pressure from various quarters. Perhaps the best approach to take is to estimate and report the standard SFA model and then discuss the degree to which the error decomposition complies with expectations.

Now assume that the regulator has solved all the foregoing problems and has measured all the components of the TFP differences between firms. Which bits should be removed? Practitioners usually argue that scale effects should be excluded, because there are usually thought to be increasing returns to scale in utilities, and because size expansion is generally not possible, at least in the short run. The issue of allocative inefficiency is quite complex. When a regulator is faced with setting a price cap in a particular industry for the first time, it often finds that some systematic allocative inefficiency is present. If the industry was previously under rate of return

---

2. The two obvious possible extremes are OLS (no inefficiency exists) and corrected OLS (no noise exists).

regulation, a degree of overcapitalization may be apparent, that is, the Averch-Johnson effect (see Averch and Johnson 1962).

Alternatively, if the industry was previously government owned, the regulator may find excess labor and excess capital because of interference from unions and politicians. Removing excess labor is not easy, but can be achieved over a five-year period. Reducing excess capital is not so easy (note that this has implications for both technical and allocative efficiency). Most capital in infrastructure is long-lived with the possible exception of some investments in the telecommunications sector. For example, if firm A has 50 percent excess capacity (that is, 50 percent higher than peak demand levels) on a supply network for a particular city, then there are two obvious ways it can address this situation: (a) wait for demand to increase, or (b) replace the asset with a smaller asset when the life of the asset has expired. When demand growth is flat and assets are relatively new, neither of these options are available. The regulator could choose to write-down the value of these assets, perhaps using an optimized replacement value approach, or alternatively, using the sale price of the firm if the firm was recently sold (and the market was not thin).

Another factor that may constrain a firm's ability to address an allocative inefficiency problem in the short run is the degree to which the input ratios are embodied in capital.[3] For example, firm A may have a lot of capital assets that are 20 years old and require more labor to maintain and operate than the types of assets that are installed today. The old assets may have been the cost-minimizing choice 20 years ago given the capital and labor prices then, but now they are not. What can the firm do in the short run?

Overall, the existence of long-lived capital assets with limited resale potential clearly makes the issue of allocative efficiency problematic. This is why some regulators have chosen to focus only on technical efficiency in comparing firms. In doing this they compare firms with similar input ratios (capital expenditures/operating expenditures) and thereby hope to make more valid comparisons. However, this is not the end of the regulatory challenge associated with efficiency measurement.

Now let us assume that the regulator has managed to measure technical efficiency and finds out that some firms are not on the frontier. Take the case where it finds that some firms are 80 percent efficient, while other firms are fully efficient (on the frontier). Now, should the regulator convert this information into a firm-specific X-factor? Consider the case where the

---

3. This is a kind of putty-clay or vintage capital argument.

average TFP growth for that sector has been 3 percent. Does the regulator set an X factor of 3 percent for the frontier firms and 7 percent (3 percent + 4 percent) for the inefficient firms? This would ensure that all firms have an incentive to be equally efficient at the end of the next five-year period. Why might this be a bad choice?

- For the regulator to insist that the frontier firms achieve 3 percent per year it must be assuming that the past TFP growth was due entirely to technical change. If part of it was due to technical efficiency improvement, say 0.5 percent, then it should perhaps only ask the frontier firms to achieve 2.5 percent.
- If 0.5 percent of this past TFP growth was due to scale effects driven by demand growth, and if the regulator believes that the new environmental laws will dampen demand growth, then perhaps it should remove another 0.5 percent from all X-factors.

However, at the beginning of the reform process, and in particular in preparation for the first cap review, most regulators will not have sufficient data to decompose the past 3 percent TFP change into these components, so let us assume it is all due to technical change and continue. This means that the inefficient firms are stuck with a 7 percent catch-up component. This is quite tough. To make sure this is reasonable, the regulator must work with the operator to identify any environmental variables (Z variables) and capital constraints we have not accounted for. This can reduce the X-factor imposed on some of the inefficient firms, but on a case by case basis. This procedure must, of course, be carried out through public audiences to avoid the real risks of corruption.

Now, five years later, what does the regulator do? Let us assume that some firms have exceeded their X-factor while others have not reached it. How can the regulator set the new X-factors and maintain incentives? For those who exceeded the X-factor, should it take away all the gains immediately or do so gradually over the next five-year period (with a firm-specific claw-back factor)? What does it do with those that did not reach their X-factor? How does the regulator keep the pressure on them, still maintain incentives, and ensure that they do not go bankrupt? Whatever it decides to do, it needs to clearly outline its strategy in the first year of the regulatory period. Predictability and consistency are critical ingredients in any incentive regulation structure. The introduction of uncertainty to the process is likely to dilute incentives.

Additional Comments

We have three additional important comments to make regarding the discussion in this chapter as follows.

- We have treated operating expenditure and capital expenditure together in this book. A number of regulators treat operating expenditure and capital expenditure separately, and only ask for operating expenditure productivity improvements while setting a "fair" rate of return on capital. This is the approach Green and Rodriguez-Pardina (1999) recommend. However, this approach can significantly dilute the incentive possibilities in CPI-X regulation. It restricts possible cost savings to operating expenditure, which is often smaller than capital expenditure in many infrastructure industries. There would also be an incentive for firms to overcapitalize (the Averch-Johnson effect) to increase profits, which would mean that the regulator must then become involved in investment planning. Furthermore, such an approach would require careful selection of productivity measures. The regulator should take care in using standard PIN TFP measures or standard efficiency measures derived using DEA or SFA, because they all include capital inputs in their measures. One option is to use an adjusted form of DEA where the efficiency measures only involve proportional reduction in the variable inputs, conditional on the levels of the fixed inputs (see Coelli, Rao, and Battese 1998, p. 172 for an example of a DEA model that can be used in this instance).
- We have not yet discussed the issue of the quality of service. Generally the regulatory system requests that firms meet certain minimum quality standards, with substantial penalties for violations; however, note that any benchmarking involving international comparisons would have to find some way of accounting for differences in quality standards across countries. One way to address this problem is for the regulatory system to explicitly define the way that quality will be taken into account in output measurement. This implies that regulators and utilities agree on the measurement of quality and on the weighting procedure used (see Saal and Parker 2001 for an interesting case study in water utilities in the United Kingdom).
- The use of the CPI in a CPI-X price cap implicitly assumes that the rate of increase in the prices the average consumer faces for food,

housing, transport, leisure, and so on is equal to the rate of increase in the input prices paid by electricity distributors (on lines, transformers, wages, interest expenses, construction costs, equipment, and so forth). If this is not true, the X-factors need to be appropriately adjusted (see, for example, the discussion in Bernstein and Sappington 1999, and for a real-life-related debate see, for instance, Office of Energy Regulation 2001).

6

Dealing with Data Concerns in Practice

Irrespective of which methodology the regulator chooses—PIN, SFA or DEA—it cannot avoid the first rule of empirical economics: garbage in = garbage out. The biggest hurdle that regulators will face is in obtaining enough data of sufficient quality to be able to conduct a robust, defensible analysis. A typical regulator will recruit an applied economist and give the economist the task of measuring efficiency in a particular network industry. Generally regulators give such people a strict deadline for completing the task, perhaps three to six months. This means the economists must often rely on secondary data sources. One of the typical main standard outcomes of a first empirical study will be a recommendation to improve the data reporting standards for the regulated industry, so that in three to five years time, when the next price cap review is due, the regulator will have a much improved dataset available for analysis.[1] In the meantime, this chapter provides some guidance on how to use the data available, drawing from examples in the various sectors in which the authors have some experience in measuring efficiency.[2] We begin with a discussion of input variables that

---

1. When setting reporting standards the regulator must keep in mind the costs firms face in collecting such data and seek to minimize these costs where possible. In an ideal world, regulators from many countries would get together and define a subset of variables that they would all agree to collect so as to improve the quality of international benchmarking studies. This would be especially valuable to small countries, where the sample sizes tend to be too small for the use of robust efficiency measurement techniques.

2. For an excellent introduction to data measurement issues in performance studies see chapter 10 in Morrison-Paul (1999). However, in reading that chapter keep in mind that the focus there is on sector-level data as opposed to firm-level data, between which some subtle differences exist.

could be used in an analysis of electricity distribution (for a comprehensive survey of recent analyses of productivity and efficiency in electricity transmission and distribution utilities see Jamasb and Pollitt 2000).

Inputs

The main categories of inputs are labor, capital, and other. To measure PIN TFP indexes we require data on both quantities and prices for each input category.

Labor

Labor can be divided into various categories, for example, unskilled, skilled, and management labor, but labor quantity is usually measured by a single aggregate variable, such as the number of full-time equivalent employees or aggregate hours worked. This is because of degrees of freedom limitations,[3] or because labor is not consistently categorized across all firms. However, keep in mind that this aggregation implicitly assumes uniform skill distributions across firms. This is usually a reasonable assumption within one country, but cross-country comparisons, say between the United States and India, could be problematic. One alternative is to measure labor quantity using total salary costs to attempt to account for differences in skill distributions across firms; however, this will also be problematic if the relative wage rates for the various categories do not reflect their relative

---

3. Degrees of freedom is the term used in regression analysis to relate the quantity of information we put into a model (observations) to the quantity of information we want to take out of it (the estimated parameters). Large degrees of freedom are good and small degrees of freedom are a worry. In regression analysis the extreme case is zero degrees of freedom, when the number of observations equals the number of parameters. In this case all data points will lie on the fitted line. There will be no deviations from the line, and hence in a production or cost frontier there will be no (measured) inefficiency. This is good news for firms and bad news for regulators. A similar thing happens in DEA, although no parameter estimates are explicitly involved. For example, we note that the addition of an extra variable to a DEA model, with the sample size held fixed, cannot cause the efficiency score of any firm to fall, but can, and often does, cause it to rise. Similarly, the removal of an observation from a sample cannot cause the efficiency score of any remaining firm to fall, but can cause it to rise. Refer to Zhang and Bartels (1998) for a good illustration of the sample size effect in electricity distribution using data from Australia, New Zealand, and Sweden.

marginal products, which is almost impossible to verify, or if the wage rates differ between firms because of geographical and other factors (see the discussion later about selecting suitable price deflators).

The price of labor can be measured in various ways. If the quantity is measured using the number of employees or hours worked, then a common approach is to measure the price of labor of each firm as the total labor costs divided by the quantity measure. This implicit labor price will pick up geographical differences in wages, assuming constant labor quality across firms; however, if labor quality (skill mix and so on) is not constant across firms, the quantity and price measures will be biased.

Capital

A discussion of the capital input could easily fill an entire book. To begin with consider the search for a measure of the quantity of capital, that is, what is the potential service flow from the capital?[4] As with labor, we can use physical quantities or monetary proxies. Physical measures are often used in international comparisons because of the many problems encountered in obtaining consistent capital valuations across different countries. These issues are discussed further later.

The main capital items in electricity distribution are lines and transformers, in ports they include the docks and the superstructure, in rail the tracks and rolling stock, and in water the pipes and the treatment stations. Other capital items would be buildings, vehicles, small machinery, computers, and so forth. However, each sector always has a couple of categories that are by far the biggest capital categories in terms of their annualized contributions to costs, and most of these inputs are far from being a homogenous commodity. For instance, in electricity distribution lines may be overhead (on poles) or underground. Poles may be wooden, concrete, or steel. The lines may be low or medium voltage (high-voltage lines are assumed to be part of the transmission network, not the distribution

---

4. Some people argue that we should try to account for capacity utilization in the capital measure. We would tend to argue that no adjustment should be made for capacity utilization, especially when dealing with cross-sectional data (see the later discussion of optimized capital measures). However, when looking at panel data and measuring TFP growth over time, one should keep the general effect of the macro-economy in mind when assessing the past performance of an industry and its likely future productivity growth prospects.

network).[5] The number of wires also differs across different parts of the network. In empirical studies the lines capital item is often proxied by a single variable, such as the length (kilometers) of network or the length of network weighted by voltage. The "braveness" of this approximation will vary from sample to sample. Transformers can also be of various sizes and types. Transformer capital is often proxied by the total sum of name-plate transformer capacity in megavolt amps. The validity of aggregating transformers of differing sizes, and hence costs per megavolt amp, is a potential criticism of this approach; however, there are fewer potential problems than with the lines measure, which is much more heterogeneous.

Given these problems with physical capital measures, using a monetary proxy for capital is tempting. With it we can aggregate all these capital items together to form a single capital variable so as to minimize the number of variables in our model and thus conserve degrees of freedom. Before we discuss how this can be done, note that in a DEA analysis there are advantages to having separate measures of the various types of capital inputs. Returning to the electricity example, this occurs when different firms deliver electricity to geographical areas with different population densities. In this instance a DEA model with separate lines and transformer measures will tend to pick out better peers (benchmark partners), because firms in sparsely populated areas will have relatively higher line to transformer ratios, and thus peer sets will have similar population densities.[6]

The construction of a value measure of capital quantity is a complex issue, and because of this we have devoted the appendix to the topic. Read this appendix carefully before collecting data for capital measurement. A firm's accounting records are an obvious source of information on capital values; however the collection process holds many traps for the unwary, including

- Divergence between accounting and economic definitions of depreciation
- Effects of inflation
- Effects of lumpy capital investment

---

5. For example, in Australia 77 kilovolts is generally used to define the boundary between transmission and distribution networks.

6. Firms in sparsely populated areas also tend to have low labor to capital and other inputs to capital ratios, and hence this nice, automatic peer selection effect will still happen to some extent, even if you only have a single aggregate measure of capital.

- Different firms using differing depreciation schedules
- Different tax rules and inflation rates in international comparison data.

This leads us to recommend the use of undepreciated replacement values as a proxy for capital quantity in the appendix, but if these are not available, we also discuss the relative merits of various second-best measures. Furthermore, we discuss various ways of calculating the user cost of capital, and thus the implicit price of capital.

Other Inputs

The other inputs variable is a catch-all category containing inputs other than labor and capital. It will contain mostly office and vehicle expenses (power, fuel, materials, services, and so on). The contribution of these individual items to total costs is generally small relative to capital and labor, and therefore they often do not warrant separate variables, though in some cases, for example, for rail and bus companies, the fuel category may be sufficiently large to warrant a separate input measure. Furthermore, different firms tend to categorize their records differently, making consistent cross-firm comparisons difficult unless regulatory data forms list specific categories.

One item that is making an increasingly large contribution to the other inputs category in many firms these days is outsourcing. When significant outsourcing of maintenance contracts occurs, the relevance of the distinction between the labor and other categories begin to blur. In such situations regulators may choose to specify a variable inputs category that contains all noncapital costs, including labor costs. Note, however, that the valid use of value measures of capital, labor, or other inputs hinges on the assumption that all firms face the same prices. If this is not true, the regulator must find suitable price deflators. This obviously becomes a significant issue when making inter-temporal and international comparisons.

Allocation of Overhead Costs and Other Issues

In several instances some costs have to be allocated across activities. First, in many sectors firms have various activities, not all of them regulated, and thus you often need to allocate various overhead costs, such as head office costs, to different activities of the same firm. For example, as well as being involved in electricity distribution, an electricity firm may also be involved in capital construction (generally of its own network), retail, and consultancy activities. When collecting data the regulator must devise a rule for allocating overheads that is fair to different types of firms and apply this rule uniformly across all firms.

Second, the regulator must judge how to draw the line between capital expenditure and maintenance expenditure. Consider again the example of electricity distributors. Is the replacement of insulators maintenance or capital investment? Is the replacement of wooden poles maintenance or investment? One could argue that pole replacement is clearly investment, yet a number of Australian electricity distributors list it on their books as maintenance. The maintenance/capital line can be drawn in any number of places, and the key issue is to draw it in the same place for all firms. Early and clear specification of such distinctions will reduce the cost of regulatory data collection and improve the quality of the results obtained in subsequent efficiency analyses.

A related, and more complex, issue is how to relate the maintenance regime in a firm to the expected life of an asset. Generally we insist on assuming the same asset lives for all firms in the sample. This is either done explicitly by replacement cost depreciation calculations, implicitly by using replacement cost as a proxy for service flow, or by using physical capital measures such as lines and transformers. Consider the example of two firms, A and B. Firm A does twice as much maintenance as firm B, and therefore can arguably expect its assets to have a longer expected life. However, if we apply the same expected asset lives to both firms, firm A will appear to be more inefficient than it actually is. Could this problem be a major issue in a dataset? In industrial countries the maintenance procedures are fairly uniform, but in some developing countries this could be an issue warranting careful attention.

Finally, one of the most obvious questions in a network industry is whether the network is an input or an output. This is one of the main sources of debate at meetings of regulators, distributors, and efficiency measurement consultants. Some representatives of electricity distribution companies have been heard to state that their job is to have the network available to carry the electricity, and that the amount of electricity carried along a particular line (10 percent or 90 percent of capacity) will not affect the cost of maintaining the line. However, engineers would be unlikely to agree with this observation. Indeed, many (if not all) published analyses of technical efficiency in electricity distribution include network length (or some related variable) as an input and not as an output.

When constructing a model for regulation purposes there is an obvious danger involved in including network length as an output variable to account for density issues. It will introduce perverse incentives by encouraging expansion of the network solely to improve a firm's efficiency score. The issue of network density is better dealt with in other ways. As already noted, the inclusion of separate measures of transformers and lines will tend to ensure that firms facing similar population densities are benchmarked against each other. Another option, also mentioned earlier, is to hold the capital input fixed when measuring efficiency. Third, if the regulator is still concerned it can define a range of population density measures and use these to see if the efficiency scores are systematically related to these factors.

Outputs

Output measures are even more complex than input measures. The obvious output measure is the quantity of electricity, of water, or of passengers transported. However, the costs involved in delivering E units of medium voltage electricity to one customer are clearly not the same as supplying E/1,000 units of low voltage electricity to each of 1,000 households, as is, partly or fully, reflected in the differential tariffs charged. Thus we seek some way of differentiating between customer types, namely, high and low volume, residential and business customers, and so on.

The most common measures of rail outputs are passenger kilometers and tonne kilometers of freight. These measures will clearly be imperfect. Some studies argue that these measures of output are heavily influenced by demand conditions, which may or may not be controllable. They therefore suggest using supply-based output measures, such as the number of seat kilometers, irrespective of whether or not they are occupied. This approach may be problematic for two reasons. First, running almost empty trains will clearly cost less in terms of fuel, ticketing, and cleaning costs than running almost full trains. Second, a model with a supply-based output measure may introduce perverse incentives for the companies to introduce services in areas of low demand at off-peak times so as to improve measured efficiency.

The relevance of the multiplicity of outputs explains why in many studies the authors use at least two output variables: electricity, gas, or water delivered and number of customers; or number of passengers and tons of freight; or number of containers. If the regulator has degrees of freedom and data to play with, then it can divide these variables into smaller categories. This has the advantage of allowing the selection of better peer firms in the efficiency comparisons.

In some cases the relative "peakiness" of demand can be a big issue. This is particularly true when comparing firms across diverse climatic regions or regions with different types of business activities. The load profile (the demand) can differ substantially between times of the day and between seasons and do so differently in different regions. The networks must be designed to deal with these peaks. Thus the regulator may also include a measure of peak supply (along with total supply and customer number variables) to account for this issue.

Some studies treat pollution as a "bad" output. This can sometimes be an important issue. For example, the installation of scrubbers to reduce emissions in power plants can be extremely costly, and can make TFP change measures appear to be low. The inclusion of bad outputs in TFP and efficiency studies is the subject of a number of recent papers, for example, Färe and others (1989).

Quality

The discussion of output measures did not consider certain possible quality differences. Reliability of supply is clearly the big quality issue in electricity distribution. Typical quality measures in industrial countries include average length of supply interruption per customer per year, delays, cancellations, and average time taken to restore supply when it has been interrupted. Collecting comparable data about supply reliability is generally difficult using existing data records because of variation in the definitions of the measures used, both between firms in some countries, and in particular between firms in different countries. Developing an internationally comparable set of definitions of reliability measures should be a priority for all regulators.

One problem with reliability measures (and the demand for output to a lesser extent) is that they can be substantially influenced by environmental events. For example, an unusually bad cyclone in one year in one geographical area may make electricity supply reliability figures look quite bad for the firms involved. Similarly, a particularly harsh winter or hot summer can cause the amount of electricity supplied by a firm to look quite good in such years. These issues indicate some of the dangers involved in using a single cross-section of data to evaluate relative performance.

In addition, a quality variable that needs to be taken into account is the technical quality of the service. The distribution of water and electricity will invariably result in losses. The design and maintenance of the network will determine how much is lost. Some studies include these losses as a variable, some include the cost of losses in the other inputs category, while other studies simply ignore it. This is one of the many judgment calls the regulator has to make.

Quality variables differ between industries. In rail the reliability of supply, that is, timeliness, is important, but safety, degree of overcrowding, frequency of services, cleanliness, and comfort of passengers are also important aspects of the quality of service. In the case of freight transport, the goods arriving undamaged is an important quality measure.

Sometimes regulators can account for some aspects of quality by carefully specifying the output measure(s). For example, two rail firms may offer quite different qualities of service. Firm A may provide large roomy seats, food and drinks served at passengers' seats, and so on, while firm B may not offer this degree of service. If this difference is reflected in the ticket prices, then a revenue measure may be a better proxy for output quantity than the traditional passenger-kilometers measure. However, if the prices differ for other reasons, such as local subsidies, the revenue measure will be biased.

Quality issues can, in some cases, be left out of the model, for example, when the regulator is analyzing a group of firms from one country where uniform minimum standards apply to all firms. The regulator can impose significant penalties for violating these standards, and then deal with TFP and pricing issues separately. However, when comparing firms that face different standards, perhaps because they are from different countries, quality will have to be considered as part of the TFP comparison. If degrees of freedom allow, and if a consistent measure of quality is available, regulators can include a quality variable; however, if it expects the effect to be limited to a few firms, or if degrees of freedom are tight, the best approach might be to omit the quality variable, and then ask the firms to discuss their individual situation with the regulator if they believe they have a case.

Quality can sometimes be an important issue in TFP measurement across time. For example, Saal and Parker's (2000) study of TFP change in the water sector in the United Kingdom showed that TFP change has been extremely slow in recent years, but that quality has improved significantly because of the large increases in minimum standards, which have incurred significant costs. Thus the use of unadjusted TFP change measures from this period would understate the potential TFP improvements (given that the quality standards are not raised again in the coming period). The Saal and Parker (2000) study suggested the use of quality-adjusted output measures to account for this effect.

Environment

Environmental variables, which efficiency studies often refer to as Z variables, are elements of the physical, cultural, or institutional environment that can affect efficiency. Like traditional input and output variables, these variables are not under the control of managers. The important variables in this category tend to be just as sector specific as quality variables. The environment for electricity is often dominated by, but not restricted to, population density, climatic, and geographic variables. The main environmental factors that can affect railways are density, topography, average haul length, average load, and government policy. In some cases the environment may also include information about the regulatory environment and other nonphysical items. Examples of typical environmental effects include low population density leading to higher costs, storms that cause fallen trees to bring down lines or stop trains, and rugged topography that makes access for maintenance teams costly.

Defining suitable measures can be tough. Even population density can be problematic, because an area with one large city and a big unpopulated area such as a desert can have the same population density as an area with many evenly scattered small and medium towns. These two configurations will clearly require different network resources.

With little effort a regulator can quickly obtain a long list of possible environmental variables to include in any model. Each firm will argue for the inclusion of the variables that will make it look better. The regulator must limit these variables to the smallest set possible, so as to control degrees of freedom. It should include only those variables that are likely to have a large effect upon a number of firms. In the case when a Z variable is likely to affect only one or two firms, the regulator can invite the firms involved to make a case for the amount by which it should adjust their efficiency score to account for this.

Prices

One of the main challenges is to obtain good input price information.[7] Given that price × quantity = cost, we need to find at least two of these three items

---

7. The regulator can also obtain output price information and look at the allocative efficiency associated with the output mix, and hence also consider profit efficiency and/or revenue efficiency. However, in infrastructure industries the output quantities and mix are rarely under the control of the firm, and thus these studies usually focus on technical efficiency and/or cost efficiency.

for each input. Because of data availability issues, the following data are often used:

- Labor: quantity and cost data obtained from each firm[8]
- Capital: replacement cost data constructed for each firm and price data based on capital price index numbers and interest rates obtained from a secondary source[9]
- Other: cost data obtained from each firm and price data based on index numbers obtained from a secondary source, such as the national statistics bureau.

Note that when an input quantity has been measured in value terms and the regulator believes that prices are constant across firms, for instance, when it has cross-sectional data and expects no geographical price variation, the price of one unit of this input is simply 1.

Depending on the method chosen, a lack of price variation between firms can be a problem. The regulator must carefully distinguish between the situation of no price variation between firms because they face the same prices, and the situation where it has no measure of price variation between firms when they do face different prices. Assuming the first case, using cost minimization DEA does not present a major problem and it can be carried out with a single price for all firms if need be.

If the regulator has no price information, but believes that all firms face the same prices, it can estimate a cost frontier, where total cost is a function of output quantities.[10] This will provide cost efficiency scores, but the regulator will not be able to decompose these into technical and allocative components. By contrast, if it has estimated such a function assuming uniform prices when this is not the case in reality, it may then end up labeling a firm as cost inefficient when it is actually efficient, but simply faces higher prices.

---

8. The implicit labor price obtained by dividing the total wage bill by the total number of employees can, in some cases, primarily indicate differences in labor force composition across firms rather than true geographical price variation.

9. Given that the user cost of capital consists of depreciation and opportunity cost, it will only vary between firms if they face different capital procurement costs and/or interest rates. This becomes more likely when dealing with panel data and/or international comparisons.

10. The dependent variable could be total costs, including both fixed (capital) costs and variable costs, or it could be just variable costs. In this latter case the regulator should include one or more variables reflecting the quantity of fixed capital as regressors.

Panel Data and International Comparisons

So far the data discussion in this chapter has not involved issues associated with time variation. What if the regulator actually has a panel of data covering several firms over several years? Access to panel data is clearly a good thing. We have already discussed the dangers of looking at just one year of data, where one weather event can have a major influence on some firms, or where a simple model may label a sensible long-term investment strategy as inefficient in the short run. With panel data we can obtain information on TFP growth and decompose it into components: technical change (shifts in the frontier), technical efficiency change (catch-up), and scale efficiency change.

Panel data provides no new data-related problems when only physical measures with consistent definitions are used; however, almost all studies involve the use of at least some value measures. For example, the use of a value measure of the other inputs variable, such as office and vehicle expenses, is usually unavoidable. Whenever we use value measures from different years we need to account for the effects of price inflation. Remember that we want the input measure to be a proxy for the physical input quantity. The choice of a good price deflator is crucial. Whenever possible, the regulator should try to avoid the use of the CPI. The average change in the prices of groceries, clothing, residential housing, vacations, and household furniture and electrical goods is usually a poor measure of the average price change in office and vehicle expenses in the electricity industry (or the price of transformers and electricity poles, engineers' wage rates, and so on). In an ideal situation the regulator will have detailed price indexes for the various input categories in the electricity industry. A second-best strategy is to use general price indexes for labor, capital, and materials in manufacturing industries, which are usually available from the national statistics bureau in each country. The CPI should be used as a last resort.

Finally, comparing a local monopoly with monopolies in comparable countries may be interesting. This is a panel data problem, but a much more complex one. Constructing datasets for international comparisons of infrastructure firms is a messy business. The data collected in different countries is generally different. This is for various reasons: historical, environmental, regulatory, and so on. The task is to collect data that is (a) relevant to local issues, (b) permits international comparison work, and (c) does not put too great an administrative burden on the firms.

Many countries collect quite similar information, but slight variations in definitions lead to comparability problems. For example, the voltage level used to distinguish transmission lines from distribution lines differs between certain countries; the division of customers into small, medium, and large categories is based on a variety of annual consumption levels in different countries; and so on. The development of an internationally consistent set of reporting standards for the principal network industries would be a significant benefit to regulators around the world.

Finally, one of the key reasons for including international firms in the performance measurement analysis is to increase the chance that the regulator has included best practice firms in the database. If the regulator's database is limited to a handful of local firms that are all equally mediocre, then the best practice level in its analysis is likely to be a long way from true best practice. Including data from other countries' firms will no doubt increase the complexity of an analysis, but the potential benefits can far outweigh the costs.

Additional Issues

One question that has generated some debate in the efficiency literature is whether environment and quality variables should be included directly in the production model, or whether regulators should only include the traditional input and output variables in the model, and then relate the efficiency scores obtained to these other variables in some type of second-stage analysis. A complicating issue is that the boundary between the variable groups is rather fuzzy. Is demand peakiness an output or an environmental issue? Is reliability of supply a quality issue or an output? The advantage of including all the variables in the production model directly is that it can help the regulator identify more appropriate peer sets. The disadvantage is that the regulator may identify no peers at all, because all firms will be unique, and hence lie on the efficiency frontier.

The inclusion of nontraditional variables into a production frontier requires some careful interpretation of the resulting efficiency scores. For example, if the regulator included an average winter temperature variable in an electricity distribution model to account for possibly higher maintenance costs in extremely cold climates, then the implication is that the intercept of the frontier now differs according to the temperature. This brings us to the issue of net versus gross efficiency measures, discussed by Coelli, Perelman, and Romano (1999) in the context of international airlines. Considering the temperature in our electricity distribution example, the regulator will obtain technical efficiency measures, which are net of the effect of temperature, if it includes the electricity variable in the model. However, if it omits the temperature variable, it obtains gross technical efficiency scores (inclusive of any temperature influence). The key issue here is to recognize that deviations from the frontier can be due to two groups of factors: those under the control of management and those not under management's control. At the end of the day the regulator needs to disentangle these two effects.

One issue that arises, irrespective of the methodology chosen, is the existence of outliers. The three main reasons for outliers are (a) typographical errors; (b) invalid observations, for example, an electricity transmission company in a sample of electricity distributors; or (c) unusual observations, for instance, an electricity distributor serving an area with a low population density. The regulator should not simply drop outliers based on some arbitrary criteria. It should correct the typographical errors (if possible), drop the invalid observations, and keep a close eye on the unusual observations as the analysis progresses.

Identifying outliers is a time-consuming but essential task. The following are some useful ways to approach the task. The regulator should

1. Check its dataset with alternative sources if possible. If it has data from a regulatory return form, it should try cross-checking what variables it can with annual reports or some other alternative data source.
2. Check its data for internal consistency. For example, if it has cost data it should ensure that the individual cost components add up to the total cost figure for each firm.
3. Look for zeros in the data, and then ask if they are sensible. Is supplying electricity with zero kilometers of lines a possibility?
4. Look at the sample means, standard deviations, minimums, maximums, and plots of all variables. Are a few data points situated a long way from the others? If so, why is this so?
5. Construct ratios of each variable over every other variable and repeat the previous exercise. Do some firms have more employees than customers? Does this make sense? Note that some partial productivity ratios can be reported in the final paper as well. The partial ratios often provide useful complementary information and can help explain the factors underlying the efficiency scores obtained from the other more comprehensive, and therefore more complex, methods.
6. Estimate some rough Cobb-Douglas OLS production, cost, and/or distance functions before estimating the final DEA or SFA model; look for large residuals and influential observations; and study them

carefully. Often the regulator will find that some observations that looked like outliers in the partial ratios look alright now, while the OLS residuals may identify some potential outliers that did not show up in the partial ratios.

Clearly, positive outliers can influence a deterministic method like DEA. One observation with an output measure that is 20 percent higher than it should be can have a nontrivial (negative) influence on the efficiency scores of many firms in the sample. In DEA counting the number of times each frontier firm is listed as a peer for another firm is a good idea. For example, if the regulator finds that one firm is being referenced as a peer by half the sample, this may be cause for some concern. It needs to take a close look at this firm. It may even try dropping this firm to look at the sensitivity of the results to its inclusion.

While only positive outliers affect DEA, both negative and positive outliers will affect SFA and OLS, thus the regulator should look carefully for both types of outliers when using the parametric methods. Furthermore, it should always assume that the data contain some errors. Finding errors in data that have already been carefully checked by the company accountant, the auditor, the regulator's office, and the research assistant of the economist doing the actual work is not uncommon.

In addition, one of the fundamental questions is determining the correct number of variables to include in the model. This question must be asked when constructing any econometric model. Consider, for example, the case of a rail study. Coming up with a long list of outputs, inputs, and environmental variables would not be difficult. Outputs could include freight and passenger trips. Freight could be divided into bulk and nonbulk, and passenger trips could be divided into short and long trips, with long trips divided into fast train and regular train services. The main inputs could include labor, fuel, length of lines, number of stations, number of locomotives, and number of passenger and freight cars. Lines could be divided into fast lines and regular lines, electrified and nonelectrified lines. Environmental variables could include the steepness of the terrain, population density, and so on. Already we have 16 possible variables, and we could easily think of some more. In a translog model this would produce a huge number of parameters to estimate, most likely more than the number of available observations. Our model estimates would be poorly estimated. We must strike a balance by aggregating some variables and omitting others. These decisions should be driven by a combination of prior knowledge of the industry and standard statistical tests. At the end of the day we must accept that our model will be imperfect. If some firms believe the model does not account for their situation, then they must make their case known to the regulator. For example, in a study of European railways Switzerland could make a case for higher fuel costs because of its steeper terrain if the model does not include a terrain variable.

A related issue is that in some cases constructing a model for the whole firm may be too difficult, because each firm may be involved in various activities. In this case the best approach may be to segment the data into activities and then run a model for each activity, as the Office of Water Services does for U.K. water companies. For example, a sample of water companies firms' activities may include water collection (dams, bores, and so on), water distribution, sewerage pipes, and/or sewerage treatment, and some firms may only be involved in a subset of these activities. Furthermore, the construction of a single model to deal properly with all the main input and output variables may be impossible, given limited numbers of observations. Thus constructing separate models for each activity may be the only sensible way to proceed, but the regulator must have good data that permit the identification of inputs and outputs for each activity (including the allocation of overheads), and must also be confident that separability between activities is a reasonable assumption.

7

Choice of Methodology

The selection of the best methodology to use in a particular application can be influenced by a number of factors, including

- The availability of data
- The likely importance of data noise
- The intended use of the results.

Data availability is always an issue. If you require a measure of TFP growth over time, then you must use whatever data are available. In some cases the availability of firm-level panel data will be extremely limited, and in such instances you may be forced to use aggregate (industry-level) time series data. In this case the methodology choice is essentially limited to the use of PIN methods such as Törnqvist or Fisher indexes.

Alternative econometric approaches, such as an OLS cost function based on time series data, are generally not recommended. To get reasonable degrees of freedom, you need a lengthy time series of data that is either not available or extends back to a period when technologies and/or data definitions differed significantly. For example, the number of free parameters in a translog cost function with two outputs, one fixed input, two variable input prices, and a time trend variable, a fairly basic list of variables, is equal to $N(N + 1)/2 = 6(6 + 1)/2 = 21$, with symmetry and homogeneity restrictions imposed. Thus to get the often quoted figure of 30 degrees of freedom or more, you require at least 51 years of data, which would take you back to the 1940s.

The inclusion of data points from more than one country may have a bearing on method choice. Obtaining consistent price and cost data across different countries can sometimes be difficult. Collecting consistent physical input and output data may be less problematic. This may encourage you to choose a primal approach using DEA or SFA over a PIN approach or a cost frontier approach using SFA, but keep in mind that these methods will not capture the effects of allocative efficiency changes.

The amount of suspected data noise can influence the choice of methodology. SFA attempts to account for noise, while DEA assumes it does not exist. Hence if you suspect that your data are of low quality, you may decide to steer away from DEA. However, you also need to take care with SFA. The standard maximum likelihood approach uses the skewness in the residuals to disentangle noise and inefficiency, thus outliers can influence this decomposition. A few large, positive residuals may convince the method that most of the error term is due to noise, while a few large, negative residuals may convince it that most of the error term is due to inefficiency.[1] One alternative is to estimate the SFA frontier using some variant of corrected OLS, using expert knowledge to adjust the intercept. However, the degree of such adjustments will clearly be a target for lobbying.

The degree of confidence you can have in efficiency scores and rankings is clearly important. Can we produce confidence intervals for our predicted efficiency scores? The answer is a qualified yes. See, for example, Kim and Schmidt (2000) for a review of the various methods that can be used in parametric models and Simar and Wilson (2000) for a discussion of the bootstrap method applied to DEA models. However, most of these methods are quite complex and have yet to become mainstream in the applied literature. Our advice is to have a look at these methods and judge for yourself whether they are feasible for you to complete within your time constraints.

The way in which you intend to use the results of your analysis will obviously have a bearing on the method chosen. Are you seeking a single, industry-wide TFP measure, or do you wish to set differential X-factors for each firm? A PIN analysis using annual aggregate data will provide an industry-wide TFP growth measure, but if you seek firm-specific X-factors then you may be interested in some form of frontier analysis, that is, apply DEA or SFA to cross-sectional or panel data.

One factor to keep in mind when assessing a firm's ability to achieve a particular X-factor is to look at the amount of new investment in capital

---

1. For example, some empirical studies have estimated separate SFA models for each cross-section in a panel dataset and noted that the percentage of the error term attributed to inefficiency can jump around from year to year in an unsatisfactory way, being near 0 in one year and near 100 percent in the next.

that is planned for that firm over the next regulatory period (usually five years). The point is that technical change can be both embodied and disembodied, and a firm that has significant investment plans, either because of demand growth or because of replacement of existing capital, will find that TFP growth is easier to achieve than a firm that has less planned investment activity.

One important issue to keep in mind in method selection is that different methods can yield different answers. For example, Ferrier and Lovell (1990), in their study of banking efficiency, found that DEA and SFA scores derived from the same dataset were essentially uncorrelated. However, this is not always the case. For example, in a study of European railways, Coelli and Perelman (1999) found a strong correlation between the scores obtained using three different methods. Either way, if possible you should apply as many methods as possible to minimize the possible impact of method selection on the results.

One potentially large source of differences in measures of TFP growth is that due to differences between shadow prices and market prices. Most standard applications of PIN methods use market prices as weights, while primal methods, such as DEA and SFA production frontiers, implicitly use shadow prices to weight the multiple inputs and outputs. Thus if you use panel data from periods when cost minimization was not the firms' objective, then the shadow prices can deviate from market prices, and the resulting TFP measures will differ from those obtained using PIN TFP growth measures constructed using market price information (see, for example, the analysis of Australian electricity generation in Coelli 2002, where the difference obtained is substantial).

An important question to ask when selecting a TFP measurement method is whether you wish to include allocative efficiency in the TFP measure? A number of authors define TFP as a purely technical measure, for example, Färe and others (1994) measure TFP growth using DEA methods and decompose it into technical change, technical efficiency change, and scale efficiency change components, but make no mention of allocative efficiency. As Coelli (2002) noted, many of the most widely cited papers on TFP do not include allocative efficiency in their TFP definitions. However, if we use PIN methods or estimate a cost frontier using OLS or SFA, we will tend to pick up the effects of changes in allocative efficiency in our TFP measure. The regulatory implications of this observation are interesting. The effects of previous regulatory regimes may have left firms with considerable scope for cost savings through allocative efficiency improvement. For example, privately-owned U.S. electricity distributors, which previously faced rate of return regulation, may have considerable excess capital capacity that they can slowly reduce through depreciation or demand growth, while Australian electricity distributors showed that they have been able to shed significant amounts of excess labor in the 1980s and1990s, a carryover from years of government ownership and strong labor unions.

Thus two obvious regulatory errors are possible. Consider the case where measured TFP growth has been 2 percent per year excluding allocative efficiency changes and 4 percent per year including it. Now if most of the allocative improvement has been made already, then insisting that firms can achieve the 4 percent growth over the next five years may be harsh. Alternatively, if more allocative slack remains to be corrected, then requesting only 2 percent annual TFP growth may be too lenient. At the end of the day, regulators are interested in the degree to which firms could be reasonably expected to reduce costs, in real terms. Thus they should be interested in allocative efficiency, but should also think carefully about the foregoing issues. In a situation where correctly implemented incentive regulation has already been in place for a number of years, we would expect the vast majority of TFP growth to be due to technical change, with technical efficiency change and allocative efficiency change playing minor roles. Therefore the selection of a TFP measurement methodology should have much less influence on the results obtained in that situation.

The orientation of a model can influence the results obtained. For example, in DEA or in SFA distance functions you can choose either an input orientation or an output orientation for the model. This is usually done on the basis of which set of variables, inputs or outputs, the firm has most control over. In the case of utilities, firms often have more control over inputs, because these firms must usually supply the level of output (electricity, water, and so on) that the public demands, and have little influence over output levels. When the technology is CRS, the choice or orientation will have no effect on the measured levels of TFP or its decomposition; however, when CRS does not hold, which is generally the case, the contribution of scale efficiency in the decomposition can be affected by the orientation. The following results apply. Under increasing returns to scale, the input-oriented scale efficiency measure will be smaller than the output-oriented scale efficiency measure, while for decreasing returns to scale the order will be the opposite. This result is predictable in DEA, because the same frontier is estimated, irrespective of the orientation chosen. However, when estimating an SFA distance function the same result is likely to occur, but one cannot say so for certain, because the position of the estimated frontier will usually differ when the orientation changes. Note also that a production frontier is an output-oriented distance function and that a cost frontier has an implicit input orientation.

Different efficiency measures can often be obtained by choosing different methods, for instance, DEA versus SFA or cost frontier versus production frontier, or by defining the variables in different ways, for example, defining labor quantity using the number of employees or the total wage bill, or defining capital using a value measure or with physical proxies. Generally the effects of these choices are not predictable in advance. For example, the efficiency scores from SFA may be larger than DEA scores because SFA accounts for noise, but they could alternatively be smaller, because DEA is more flexible and hence fits the data more tightly. A firm wishing to "look good" could try a number of different methods and variable definitions and choose the most favorable results. If all parties agree that a PIN measure (such as, Törnqvist) is the "correct" TFP measure, then only variable definitions can affect the TFP measures, while method choice will only affect the decomposition.

Finally, the scale assumptions (CRS or VRS) of the model can influence results. When comparing relative efficiency at one point in time, this issue will be crucial, given that regulators are often required to compare the efficiency of groups of firms with different scales of operation (which they generally are unable to modify). However, when looking at changes over time, scale is likely to be less of an issue, but in some cases scale changes may be important, for example, in the telecommunications industry in developing countries. In situations when demand is growing fast, the regulator should take care not to simply ask for an X-factor based on some international average TFP measure, because the local firm may then reap considerable profits from scale efficiency improvements. However, on the other side of the coin, the regulator should also take care not to use the historical TFP growth of a firm (based on data from a demand growth phase) to set TFP growth targets after the market has matured and demand growth has reduced.

A number of regulators have already applied these techniques in constructing incentive regulation structures. Yardstick competition is used in the United Kingdom in the water and electricity sectors. Australia has implemented international benchmarks to assess the comparison of some of its own operators. All the key results are available on the web sites of the regulators in these countries (provided earlier). In addition to easing the dissemination of best practice in the field, the way this information is disseminated in these countries helps improve the accountability of both operators and regulators. It helps inform users and allows them to compare prices and costs across regions and find out more about the sources of differences. In addition, it also increases the accountability of the regulator, as it reduces the risks that the regulator may discriminate unfairly in favor of any specific operator, thereby reducing the risks of capture or corruption.

To date few developing countries have relied on this form of competition explicitly. Mexico is currently trying to adapt it to its ports sector and various other Latin American countries are expected to participate in a larger project that would allow regulators to compare performance internationally.[2] In Brazil, where water utilities are either municipal or provincial, a database has recently been put together to allow comparative performance assessments, and will be used by the new regulator to assess the relative performance of the main water utilities.

A recent study by Rodriguez-Pardina and Rossi (1999b) applied to electricity distribution companies in Latin America showed how these comparative performance assessments can also be done with international data and provides useful information to each national regulator on the relative efficiency of the operators under their control. Similar studies have been carried out for international comparisons of water utilities for Africa (Estache and Kouassi 2002) and Asia (Estache and Rossi 2002).

---

2. See Estache, Gonzalez, and Trujillo (2001) for a description of Mexico's experience in the port sector and Crampes, Diette, and Estache (1990) for an early assessment of comparative assessments of water utilities in Brazil

8

Concluding Comments

When a regulator uses a method such as DEA or SFA to measure the efficiency of individual firms and plans to use this information as part of the process of setting firm-specific X-factors, the inefficient firms will put the empirical results under intense scrutiny. The regulator may want to be reasonable, but firm. This book has shown that the areas of uncertainty can be significant and that the best a regulator should expect is to be able to put a number on the table for discussion; however, that number should be robust.

One way to do this is to demonstrate the sensitivity of the efficiency scores to various changes in the model. You could start by trying models with different sets of variables, for example, using labor measured in physical or value units and electricity output divided into residential and business customers. You could also try different methodologies, such as PIN, DEA, or SFA. Furthermore, you can try dropping some of the frontier (efficient) firms to see how stable the frontier is. If all these activities have little influence on the efficiency score, then the largest efficiency score obtained for each firm can be used in a fairly confident manner.

When conducting your empirical analysis of performance, be sure to allow plenty of time for feedback and comments from the stakeholders, that is, the development of the efficiency models should be an inclusive process. You should show the firms and other stakeholders draft versions of the efficiency analyses and encourage them to criticize the variables selected, the way the variables have been defined and measured, and so on. If the firms believe a better model could be estimated, they should be encouraged to supply any extra data that are needed that would permit the new analysis. It is important that the stakeholders see the analysis as an iterative process and not as a "take it or leave it" situation.

Regulators that are embarking on this type of analysis for the first time should make contact with those regulators who have had experience in this area, for example, those in Australia, Scandinavia, and the United Kingdom, and learn from their experiences and mistakes. Regulators should also attempt to establish such international contacts so they can discuss ways in which they can collect data on a more consistent basis across national boundaries. One of the biggest problems many small countries face is that they have relatively few firms that can be used for efficiency comparisons, and thus to obtain robust efficiency measures regulators from

---

Box 8.1. *Examples of Recent Performance Studies*

- Electricity industry studies: Atkinson and Halvorsen (1980, 1984); Bagdadioglu, Price, and Weyman-Jones (1996); Burns and others (2000); Byrnes, Grosskoft, and Hayes (1986); Coelli (2002); Estache, Rossi, and Ruzzier (2002); Førsund and Kittelsen (1998); Hjalmarsson and Viederpass (1992a,b); Jamasb and Pollitt (2000); Kumbhakar and Hjalmarsson (1998); Pollitt (1995); Roberts (1986); Rodriguez-Pardina and Rossi (1999a); Salvanes and Tjotta (1994); Weyman-Jones (1991, 1992); Weyman-Jones and Burns (1996); Zhang and Bartels (1998).
- Gas industry studies: Carrington, Coelli, and Groom (2002); Kim and others (1999); Rodriguez-Pardina and Rossi (1999b); Rossi (2001); Rushdi (1994), Waddams-Price and Weyman-Jones (1996).
- Port studies: Coto, Baños, and Rodríguez (2000); Cullinane and Khanna (1998); Estache, Gonzalez, and Trujillo (2001); Liu (1995); Martinez and others (1999); Roll and Hayuth (1993); Tongzon (2001).
- Railways studies: Caves and Christensen (1980); Caves, Christensen, and Swanson (1981); Coelli and Perelman (1999, 2000); Cowie and Riddington (1996); Dodgson (1985, 1994); Estache, Gonzalez, and Trujillo (forthcoming); Gathon and Perelman (1992); Nash (1985); Perelman and Pestieau (1988).
- Telecommunications studies: Das (2000); de Boer (1996); Fuss (1994); Giokas and Pentzaropolulos (2000); Norsworthy and Tsai (1999); Rushdi (2000); Sueyoshi (1994, 1997).
- Water industry studies: Ashton (2000); Bhattacharyya, Harris, and Rangesan (1995); Crain and Zardkoohi (1978); Crampes, Diette, and Estache (1990); Estache and Kouassi (2002); Estache and Rossi (2002); Feigenbaum and Teeples (1984); Fox and Hofler (1986); Hunt and Lynk (1995); Saal and Parker (2000).

such countries must often seek data on firms from other countries to supplement their databases. Collecting international data using consistent variable definitions will be extremely useful in these situations.

When selecting variables for inclusion in your production model do not try to include every possible minor variable. This will produce a model in which every firm looks fully efficient simply because it is unique in some way. Include only the main input and output variables, plus any environmental variables that are likely to have a significant effect on most firms. Once you have obtained the efficiency measures from this model, use the measures as a starting point for discussions between the regulator and the regulated firm. If the firms believe that they are unique in some way, the onus should be on them to make a case and quantify the extra costs associated with their particular situation.

Often the best way to learn about any task is to learn from the experiences of others (see box 8.1). Many performance studies have been conducted in recent years that you can read and learn from; however, while reading be sure to maintain a critical perspective. Some of these studies use sets of input and output variables that are far from optimal, primarily because the authors faced various types of data constraints. Keep this in mind when you embark on your empirical analysis. Furthermore, if you discover that you also face data constraints, be open and honest about the limitations of your analysis, use your performance measures in a conservative fashion, and ensure that the regulator quickly amends firms' data reporting requirements. This will ensure that future efficiency studies are less affected by data limitations, and hence provide better-quality information for use in future regulatory determinations.

Appendix: Capital Measurement

Measuring the quantity, price, and cost of capital is challenging, because capital is a durable input. Unlike other inputs such as labor and fuel, which are generally purchased and consumed within a particular accounting period, say a year, capital is purchased during one period and then supplies services over many periods. Consider the example of a telecommunications company that has purchased a piece of switching equipment that has an expected life of 20 years. The equipment is purchased and installed in year 1 and continues to supply services for another 19 years. So the question we face in our attempt to measure the productivity and efficiency of this firm is: What is the appropriate measure of the quantity and price (and hence cost) of capital in each of these 20 years? We will begin with a discussion that assumes that we have all information available to us. Following this we will discuss the more usual situation where we have limited information.

Capital Quantity

The quantity of capital should reflect the potential service flow that can be derived from the capital equipment in each year. Expecting the potential service flow to be quite similar in each of the 20 years is reasonable, though more down time could be required in the latter years of the asset's life as more maintenance is required. Hence the potential service flow in year 20 could be 5 or 10 percent below that in year 1 (an engineer could provide advice on this matter). In any case, it is often reasonable to assume that the potential service flow will be quite similar from one year to the next.[1] For this reason accountants have often used the method of straight-line depreciation to distribute the purchase cost of an asset over its service life. Thus a piece of equipment that is purchased for US$1,000, which has an expected life of 20 years and an expected scrap value of zero, could be depreciated in the accounts by US$50 per year for the 20-year period.

Thus the depreciation expenses reported in a firm's accounts may provide a good proxy for the quantity of capital each firm uses each year. However, this measure might be problematic because

- Price inflation will make the quantities (that is, the depreciation cost) of new capital items appear larger than identical capital items purchased in previous years.
- Different firms could assume different asset lives or use different depreciation patterns, such as declining balance, or use accelerated depreciation to minimize tax payments.

These problems can be particularly large when dealing with firm-level data in infrastructure industries, where capital investment patterns can be extremely lumpy and where these patterns differ substantially between firms. This factor results in biases in the relative estimates of capital quantity for a particular firm through time, and also produces biased estimates across a group of firms at one point in time.

We can overcome these problems if we have a full history of investment expenditures for each firm and a good index or indexes of price inflation for capital inputs over this period. We can then convert all past nominal investments into constant price values and then apply the same depreciation rules to the constant price undepreciated capital stocks of each firm to obtain good comparable measures of capital quantities.

We could perform these calculations at various levels of aggregation depending on the amount of data and the amount of time available. For example, we could divide capital expenditure into two categories, buildings and fixed structures and machinery and equipment, and then apply different asset lives, and thus different depreciation rates to each category, and so on. If the amount of data (or time) is limited, we can apply an average depreciation schedule to the aggregate capital measures; however, we

---

1. Note that when we use physical proxies as our capital measures, such as network length and transformer capacity, we are also implicitly assuming that the service flow of the asset is not affected by its age.

would need to look out for any substantial variations in capital composition across firms. If substantial differences do exist, the application of a uniform asset life to all firms will provide upward biased estimates of the quantity of capital used by those firms with higher proportions of long-life assets, that is, with more buildings and fixed structures.

The foregoing discussion assumed that we had all the data we could want. In reality, data are often limited. In situations in which we do not have investment history data, we can consider other ways of measuring the quantity of capital, namely:

- Replacement value
- Optimized replacement value
- Sale value
- Nominal (undepreciated) capital stock
- Nominal depreciated capital stock
- Depreciated replacement value.

Replacement Value

The undepreciated replacement value of the capital stock held by a firm should, in theory, be equivalent to the value of the undepreciated constant price capital stock obtained by deflating a historical investment series as described earlier. However, estimating the replacement value of each item of capital in each firm will be a costly and time-consuming exercise. When a new regulatory regime is due to be introduced, assuming that sufficient time and money are available, the regulator can commission a consulting company to value the assets of all firms. Once this valuation has been made for a particular year, the regulator can then use this valuation and subsequent annual information on new investment and retirements to update this valuation each year.

Optimized Replacement Value

Some regulators in Australia have sought to adjust the standard replacement value measures so as not to penalize new owners or managers for past investment mistakes. Thus they have set out to measure the optimized replacement value of each asset in each firm. The optimized capital value is the value of the asset that you would replace an asset with today, given all you now know about the industry (expected future demand, regulatory structure, and so on). This concept is best explained with a simple example.

Consider the case where an electricity distribution firm has sufficient capital capacity in lines and transformers to supply double the current or expected peak demand to a particular suburb of a city. This may have resulted from poor demand forecasting, gold-plating, or other reasons; but the historical reason is of little importance at this stage. As long as we can argue that the current owners or managers did not make this investment decision, we could argue that we should specify an optimized capital value equal to approximately one-half of the replacement value of the capital that is actually installed. However, we generally recommend avoiding the temptation to play around with optimized capital values, mostly because the amount of subjective (and expensive) judgment involved is substantial. Problems can occur even when the same team does all the evaluations at one point in time, but when different teams are used, as is generally unavoidable in international comparisons, the data are often difficult to compare.

Sale Price

If a business has recently been sold in the market for a particular price, we can argue that the value of the capital stock should be reflected in the sale price; however, this may or may not be a good valuation and depends a good deal on how competitive the sale process was. The generally small number of serious bids received in many sales is often a cause for some concern.

Nominal Undepreciated Capital Stock

The nominal undepreciated capital stock is routinely reported in annual accounts. This measure will be biased when inflation is nonzero and investment is lumpy. In periods of high inflation (above 10 percent per year) the degree of bias can be substantial and can fluctuate widely, both between firms and from year to year.

Nominal Depreciated Capital Stock

The nominal depreciated capital stock will be an even poorer measure of the quantity of capital than nominal undepreciated capital stock, because the effects of depreciation will magnify the effects of lumpy capital investment.

Depreciated Replacement Value

The depreciated replacement value will be a better measure than nominal depreciated capital stock, because the effects of inflation have been removed; however, the effects of depreciation on lumpy capital investment will introduce biases. An example is presented later when we compare the biases introduced by these latter three measures when capital investment is lumpy.

Capital Cost

The cost of capital consists of depreciation and interest expenses.[2] The interest expenses should include both the cost of debt and the forgone interest on equity. Cost information is often quite important in productivity and efficiency studies. Cost shares are required to construct Törnqvist and Fisher TFP indexes and prices are needed to calculate allocative efficiency. Note, however, that an analysis of technical efficiency does not require cost information.

An obvious measure of the depreciation cost is that presented in the accounts, but the interest expenses reported in the accounts will only reflect the cost of debt and ignore the implicit (forgone opportunity) cost of equity. Thus we could calculate the interest costs by applying a suitable interest rate (or rate of return) to the depreciated capital stock reported in the accounts. The rate of return could take account of the percentage of debt and equity. This is often done using the weighted average cost of capital (WACC):

$$WACC = [(1 - g) \times r_e] + [g \times r_d],$$

where g is the leverage, which is equal to debt/(debt + equity), r_d is the cost of debt finance, and r_e is the cost of equity. The cost of equity is often calculated using the capital asset pricing model (CAPM):

$$CAPM = r_e = r_f + \beta_e \times (r_m - r_f),$$

---

2. Some studies include maintenance expenses as a component of capital costs, but most do not because distinguishing between such expenses in the accounts is often not possible. Furthermore, differing degrees of maintenance work between firms may imply different asset lives. Thus the calculation of depreciation costs on the assumption that all firms have identical asset lives may be disadvantageous for those firms that carry out more maintenance. A related comment could be made when the utilization rates differ significantly between firms: higher utilization rates could imply shorter asset lives.

where r_f is the risk-free return, r_m is the market return, and β_e is the equity beta reflecting the degree of risk. In regulated industries the size of β_e can vary with the incentive characteristics of the regulatory structure, for example, it could move from 0.3 to 0.7 as one moves from low-incentive to high-incentive situations (see Green and Rodriguez-Pardina 1999 for more discussion of WACC and CAPM issues).

The measures of depreciation costs and interest costs suggested earlier are derived from nominal values, and thus will reflect the actual total costs the firm faces over the life of the asset. However, the depreciation costs decline in real terms over the life of the asset, and the interest costs will decline both in nominal and real terms. When investment is lumpy, which is usually the case in firm-level data, the measured cost of capital will tend to fluctuate.[3] One alternative approach, which can remove the fluctuations caused by inflation, is to calculate depreciation and interest expenses based on the depreciated replacement value of the capital stock. Regulators often adopt this approach when calculating allowable capital costs; however, it will generally provide an overstatement of the total cost of the asset. In example 1 this results in a 22 percent overstatement of the present value cost of the asset.

Example 1

In the example presented in table A1 we consider investment in an asset that has a purchase price of US$1,000 dollars in year 0, a life of 20 years, and a scrap value of zero. We assume straight-line depreciation, an inflation rate of 3 percent, and a nominal interest rate of 9.5 percent, which is also the discount factor used in present value calculations.[4] The firm also uses labor whose real wage rate (in year 0 dollars) is US$10 per hour in every year. We assume that the firm expected these wage rates in year 0.[5] Thus the firm would have based its investment decisions on the discounted

---

3. That is, even when the quantity of capital held by the firm is constant and the real prices of capital are constant, the cost of capital held by the firm will fall, implying that the price of capital the firm faces has fallen.

4. These need not be the same. We experimented with discount factors as high as 15 percent, but found no major changes to our conclusions.

5. Thus we assume that ex ante price expectations are realized in the ex post prices. In reality, a firm will base its investment decisions on expected prices, which may or may not be realized, and thus an investment that is optimal ex ante can appear to be suboptimal ex post.

Table A.1. Present Value Calculations of Capital Costs

1	2	3	4	5	6	7	8	9	10	11	12	Using replacement values		
												13	14	15
Year of obser- vation	Depre- ciation	Depre- ciated value	Interest expenses	Deprecia- tion and interest expenses	PV discount factor	PV deprecia- tion and interest	Inflation index	Real wage rate	Nominal wage rate	Capital/ labor price ratio	PV of wages	Deprecia- tion and interest	Capital/ labor price ratio	PV deprecia- tion and interest
0		1,000			1.00		1.00							
1	50	950	95.00	145.00	1.10	132.42	1.03	10.00	10.30	14.08	9.41	149.35	14.50	136.39
2	50	900	90.25	140.25	1.20	116.97	1.06	10.00	10.61	13.22	8.85	148.79	14.03	124.09
3	50	850	85.50	135.50	1.31	103.20	1.09	10.00	10.93	12.40	8.32	148.06	13.55	112.77
4	50	800	80.75	130.75	1.44	90.95	1.13	10.00	11.26	11.62	7.83	147.16	13.08	102.36
5	50	750	76.00	126.00	1.57	80.04	1.16	10.00	11.59	10.87	7.36	146.07	12.60	92.79
6	50	700	71.25	121.25	1.72	70.34	1.19	10.00	11.94	10.15	6.93	144.78	12.13	83.99
7	50	650	66.50	116.50	1.89	61.72	1.23	10.00	12.30	9.47	6.52	143.28	11.65	75.91
8	50	600	61.75	111.75	2.07	54.07	1.27	10.00	12.67	8.82	6.13	141.56	11.18	68.49
9	50	550	57.00	107.00	2.26	47.28	1.30	10.00	13.05	8.20	5.77	139.61	10.70	61.69
10	50	500	52.25	102.25	2.48	41.26	1.34	10.00	13.44	7.61	5.42	137.42	10.23	55.45
11	50	450	47.50	97.50	2.71	35.93	1.38	10.00	13.84	7.04	5.10	134.96	9.75	49.73
12	50	400	42.75	92.75	2.97	31.21	1.43	10.00	14.26	6.51	4.80	132.24	9.28	44.50
13	50	350	38.00	88.00	3.25	27.05	1.47	10.00	14.69	5.99	4.51	129.23	8.80	39.72
14	50	300	33.25	83.25	3.56	23.37	1.51	10.00	15.13	5.50	4.25	125.92	8.33	35.34
15	50	250	28.50	78.50	3.90	20.12	1.56	10.00	15.58	5.04	3.99	122.30	7.85	31.35
16	50	200	23.75	73.75	4.27	17.26	1.60	10.00	16.05	4.60	3.76	118.35	7.38	27.70
17	50	150	19.00	69.00	4.68	14.75	1.65	10.00	16.53	4.17	3.53	114.05	6.90	24.38
18	50	100	14.25	64.25	5.12	12.54	1.70	10.00	17.02	3.77	3.32	109.38	6.43	21.35
19	50	50	9.50	59.50	5.61	10.61	1.75	10.00	17.54	3.39	3.13	104.33	5.95	18.60
20	50	0	4.75	54.75	6.14	8.91	1.81	10.00	18.06	3.03	2.94	98.88	5.48	16.10
PV						1,000.00					111.86			1,222.72

PV Present value.

values of per unit capital and labor costs. The present value of costs will be minimized by equating this price ratio with the ratio of the marginal products of capital and labor.

Let us now consider the contents of table A1 column by column. The year of observation is in column 1 and the depreciation of $50 per year is in column 2. Column 3 contains the depreciated value of the asset, while column 4 shows the interest expenses, which are 9.5 percent of the opening value of the asset. In column 5 we have the sum of depreciation and interest expenses. Note that these fall from US$145 to US$54.75 over the life of the asset, because of the declining interest expenses due to the depreciating value of the asset. Also keep in mind that all values in columns 1 to 5 are in nominal prices, and hence will also decrease in real terms as time passes because of the effects of inflation.

As stated earlier, the rational firm will use present value calculations to make decisions about the optimal mix of capital and labor. Thus in column 6 we present the present value discount factor, assuming a discount rate of 9.5 percent per year. In column 7 we list the present values of the nominal depreciation and interest expenses obtained by deflating column 5 by column 6. The sum of these present values is equal to the original purchase price of the asset, as we would expect.[6] In columns 8 to 10 we present information on wages. In column 8 we present the inflation discount factor, in column 9 the real wage rate of US$10 per hour, and in column 10 the nominal wage rate obtained by multiplying columns 8 and 9.

In column 11 we present the capital/labor price ratio, which is the ratio of columns 5 and 10. This is the price ratio we would observe if we used column 5 as our cost of capital. The measured price ratio has fallen dramatically over the 20-year period from 14.08 to 3.03. Now in reality, the price ratio has not changed at all. A better measure of the relative prices of labor and capital would be the ratio of the present values. From column 12 we see that the sum of the present values of wages is US$111.86. Thus the ratio of the present value of a unit of capital to the present value of a unit of labor is equal to $1,000/111.86 = 8.94$. This is the type of ratio the firm would have used to make its original investment decision, it is the price ratio we should use to assess the allocative efficiency of the firm,[7] and it is the price

---

6. This would not be the case if we chose a discount factor that differed from the nominal interest rate.

7. This comment is relevant because we have assumed no change in relative prices during the 20-year period. If prices did change, and if the firm did not anticipate these changes, then we must choose between ex post and ex ante prices in assessing allocative efficiency.

ratio we should use to calculate the cost shares for use in our Törnqvist or Fisher TFP index.[8]

However, the foregoing present value calculations will never be a practical option. So what can we do to minimize these "s-bend" effects in capital costs? We can think of three possibilities, namely:

- Use the nominal figures from the accounts and hope the effect is small.
- Aggregate the firm-level data and calculate an industry-level capital quantity and cost, which will provide an implicit industry-level capital price, and then use this price and the firm-level quantity data to calculate the firm-level capital costs. Further discussion of this option is provided in our later discussion of price calculation.
- Use replacement values to calculate depreciation and interest expenses.

We noted earlier that many regulators use replacement values instead of nominal values in calculating depreciation and interest expenses. In columns 13 to 15 of table A1 we have looked at the impact of doing this. In column 13 we have estimated the replacement value depreciation and interest expenses by multiplying the nominal depreciation and interest expenses in column 5 by the inflation index in column 8. Thus by removing the inflation effect we see much less variation in capital costs in column 13. In column 14 we present the implied capital/labor price ratio, where we see that this ratio does not vary as much as that in column 11, but it still does vary by a factor of almost 3 over the life of the asset. Finally, in column 15 we calculate the present values and note that the sum of the present values overstates the purchase price by 22 percent. Thus in terms of productivity and efficiency studies, the use of replacement values could lead to the overstatement of average capital prices, and hence to biased estimates of TFP and allocative efficiency. Furthermore, when these capital cost calculations are used in rate of return regulatory calculations, they will obviously allow the regulated firm to more than recover the costs of capital.

---

8. Note that we have also done some rough experiments looking at the effects of accelerated depreciation allowances on these figures. This had the expected effects of increasing the price of capital in early periods and decreasing the price in later periods, with an overall reduction in the after tax present value of the cost of the capital item.

Overall, the calculations presented in table A1 are dramatic. They would be applicable if the firm completely renewed all its capital once every 20 years. In reality, most firms in infrastructure industries invest more regularly than that, and thus we would not see such dramatic year to year changes in most firms. However, a quick study of the age profiles of assets across infrastructure firms in any country will generally reveal quite different age profiles across firms. These are generally due to a range of historical factors relating to varying development patterns in different areas, political issues, and so on. Thus this is an issue that should never be underestimated. We attempt to illustrate this in the next example.

Example 2

In the example in table A2 we consider three electricity distribution firms: firm A, firm B, and firm C. At the end of year 40 they are identical in every respect. The only capital they have is in distribution lines (we assume this to keep it simple). They have each invested in 2.5 kilometers (km) of lines per year for 40 years. Thus in year 40 they all have 100 km of lines with identical age profiles, which have identical book values. We assume that each firm faces the same input prices, which increase at 3 percent per year. Each firm uses identical straight-line depreciation rules, where the assumed life of an asset is 40 years and the scrap value is zero.

Over the 10 years from year 41 to year 50 all three firms increase their stock of capital from 100 to 105 km. This involves the installation of 30 km of new lines and the retirement of 25 km of existing lines that were installed in years 1 to 10. The only difference between the three firms is that we set them different investment paths over this 10-year period. Firm A conducts investment in a smooth way, installing 3 new km each year, while firm B does most investment in the first few years and firm C does most investment in the final few years.

Now as all three firms have the same length of lines in the final year (year 50), we would ideally like to have a capital quantity (and cost and price) measure that is identical across these three firms. We look at four possible measures of capital quantity in this table:[9]

---

9. All four measures of capital quantity considered here are stock measures. If we assume identical depreciation rates, these will be directly proportional to the implied depreciation values.

- Nominal undepreciated stock
- Nominal depreciated stock
- Replacement value
- Depreciated replacement value.

As we would expect, the replacement value provides identical measures for all three firms; however, the other three measures are not identical. They overstate the quantity of capital for the firm that invested late in the period and understate it for the firm that invested early in the period. The nominal undepreciated capital stock provides a 8.1 percent difference because of the effects of inflation. In periods when inflation is well above 3 percent, this difference will clearly be much larger.[10] The use of a nominal depreciated capital stock is substantially worse. Here we find a difference of almost 25 percent between firms B and C. The combined effects of depreciation and inflation have caused this disparity. The fourth measure, depreciated replacement value, is an improvement over this measure, with only a 9.3 percent gap, because the effects of inflation have been removed.

The purpose of the example in table A2 was to provide a conservative illustration of the possible biases in various alternative measures of capital quantity. It is fairly clear that the use of the nominal depreciated capital stock, which is often used in applied studies, should be avoided at all costs. It is also clear that undepreciated replacement value, if available, is the optimal choice. However, if it is not available, you can choose either the nominal undepreciated stock or the depreciated replacement cost without introducing major biases (in this example). The nominal undepreciated stock is routinely reported in firms' accounts, and hence is likely to be the easiest information to obtain. However, avoid using this measure when dealing with data in which there are periods of high inflation, because nominal figures will be greatly distorted.

One final point about example 2 is that the only thing that we assumed differed between the firms was the pattern of investment over the most recent 10-year period. In reality, many more things could vary, including the depreciation methods used by each firm (declining balance or straight-line); the assumed lives of each type of asset; the use of accelerated depreciation

---

10. When an inflation rate of 10 percent per year was considered in table A2 we calculated differences in capital valuations of 34 and 73 percent in the nominal and depreciated nominal values, respectively.

Table A.2. Effects of Lumpy Capital Investment

Number of years since operation start	New km	Retired km of distribution lines	Total km of distribution lines	Inflation index	Unit price	Investment value of new km	Value of retired lines	Nominal undepreciated stock	Nominal depreciation	Nominal depreciated stock	Nominal interest	Nominal depreciation and interest	Replacement value	Depreciated km	Depreciated replacement value
Firm A															
40			100.0	1.000	100			5,952		3,474			10,000	48.750	4,875
41	3	2.5	100.5	1.030	103	309	79	6,182	155	3,629	345	499	10,352	49.238	5,071
42	3	2.5	101.0	1.061	106	318	81	6,419	160	3,787	360	520	10,715	49.713	5,274
43	3	2.5	101.5	1.093	109	328	84	6,663	167	3,948	375	542	11,091	50.175	5,483
44	3	2.5	102.0	1.126	113	338	86	6,915	173	4,113	391	564	11,480	50.625	5,698
45	3	2.5	102.5	1.159	116	348	89	7,173	179	4,281	407	586	11,883	51.063	5,920
46	3	2.5	103.0	1.194	119	358	92	7,440	186	4,453	423	609	12,299	51.488	6,148
47	3	2.5	103.5	1.230	123	369	94	7,715	193	4,630	440	633	12,729	51.900	6,383
48	3	2.5	104.0	1.267	127	380	97	7,998	200	4,810	457	657	13,174	52.300	6,625
49	3	2.5	104.5	1.305	130	391	100	8,289	207	4,994	474	682	13,635	52.688	6,875
50	3	2.5	105.0	1.344	134	403	103	8,589	215	5,182	492	707	14,111	53.063	7,131
Firm B															
40			100.0	1.000	100			5,952		3,474			10,000	48.750	4,875
41	3	2.5	100.5	1.030	103	309	79	6,182	155	3,629	345	499	10,352	49.238	5,071
42	15	2.5	113.0	1.061	106	1,591	81	7,692	192	5,028	478	670	11,988	61.413	6,515
43	12	2.5	122.5	1.093	109	1,311	84	8,920	223	6,116	581	804	13,386	70.350	7,687
44	0	2.5	120.0	1.126	113	0	86	8,833	221	5,895	560	781	13,506	67.350	7,580
45	0	2.5	117.5	1.159	116	0	89	8,745	219	5,677	539	758	13,621	64.413	7,467
46	0	2.5	115.0	1.194	119	0	92	8,653	216	5,460	519	735	13,732	61.538	7,348
47	0	2.5	112.5	1.230	123	0	94	8,559	214	5,247	498	712	13,836	58.725	7,222
48	0	2.5	110.0	1.267	127	0	97	8,462	212	5,035	478	690	13,934	55.975	7,091
49	0	2.5	107.5	1.305	130	0	100	8,362	209	4,826	458	668	14,026	53.288	6,953
50	0	2.5	105.0	1.344	134	0	103	8,259	206	4,619	439	645	14,111	50.663	6,809

Firm C

40			100.0	1.000	100			5,952		3,474			10,000	48.750	4,875
41	3	2.5	100.5	1.030	103	309	79	6,182	155	3,629	345	499	10,352	49.238	5,071
42	0	2.5	98.0	1.061	106	0	81	6,101	153	3,476	330	483	10,397	46.788	4,964
43	0	2.5	95.5	1.093	109	0	84	6,017	150	3,326	316	466	10,436	44.400	4,852
44	0	2.5	93.0	1.126	113	0	86	5,931	148	3,178	302	450	10,467	42.075	4,736
45	0	2.5	90.5	1.159	116	0	89	5,842	146	3,032	288	434	10,491	39.813	4,615
46	0	2.5	88.0	1.194	119	0	92	5,750	144	2,888	274	418	10,508	37.613	4,491
47	0	2.5	85.5	1.230	123	0	94	5,656	141	2,747	261	402	10,515	35.475	4,363
48	0	2.5	83.0	1.267	127	0	97	5,559	139	2,608	248	387	10,514	33.400	4,231
49	15	2.5	95.5	1.305	130	1,957	100	7,416	185	4,379	416	601	12,461	46.013	6,004
50	12	2.5	105.0	1.344	134	1,613	103	8,926	223	5,769	548	771	14,111	55.388	7,444
Ratio of smallest to largest valuation in year 50:								1.081		1.249			1.000		1.093

or not; the differences in prices and inflation rates different firms face, especially in international comparison work; and so on.

If you have limited time or money and are therefore obliged to use suboptimal measures from accounting records, do try to check for anomalies by making a careful comparison between these measures and any physical capital measures you may have. Make scatter plots of value versus length of lines or transformer capacity and look for strange observations. You may also consider estimating a rough regression equation of your value measures of capital against a number of these variables and look for outliers and so on.

Capital Prices

Once we have measures of capital quantity and cost, we can calculate capital prices residually using the relationship that cost = quantity × price, and hence that price = cost/quantity. However, before we do this we must ask ourselves an important question: Do we believe that the firms in our sample face different prices? If so, why is this? Why is it that some firms pay lower interest rates or lower prices on a meter of cable or on a particular construction job? Perhaps the measured price differences are actually due to inefficiency in the installation and/or construction of new capital, which is often done by another arm of the same company. Allowing firms to have different capital prices may provide a temptation for some firms to use this to pass through above average costs to the consumer.

If we believe that the firms in our sample actually face identical capital prices, then perhaps we should impose this? This can be done by calculating an industry-level price using aggregates of our firm-level data on costs and quantities, and then using this industry-level price (and the firm-level quantity measures) to calculate the implicit costs of each firm. This will also reduce the s-bend capital cost measurement problem discussed earlier.

References

The word "processed" describes informally reproduced works that may not be commonly available through libraries.

Agrell, P. J., P. Bogetoft, and J. Tind. 2002. "Incentive Plans for Productive Efficiency, Innovation, and Learning." *International Journal of Production Economics* 78:1–11.

Armstrong, M., S. Cowan, and J. Vickers. 1994. *Regulatory Reform: Economic Analysis and British Experience*. Cambridge, Massachusetts: MIT Press.

Ashton, J. K. 2000. "Cost Efficiency in the U.K.'s Water and Sewerage Industry." *Applied Economic Letters* 7: 455–58.

Atkinson, S. E., and R. Halvorsen. 1980. "A Test of Relative and Absolute Price Efficiency in Regulated Utilities." *Review of Economics and Statistics* 62(1): 81–88.

———. 1984. "Parametric Efficiency Tests, Economies of Scale, and Input Demand in U.S. Electric Power Generation." *International Economic Review* 25(3): 647–62.

Averch, H., and L. L. Johnson. 1962. "Behavior of the Firm under a Regulatory Constraint." *American Economic Review* 52(5): 1053–69.

Bagdadioglu, N., C. Price, and T. Weyman-Jones. 1996. "Efficiency and Ownership in Electricity Distribution: A Nonparametric Model of the Turkish Experience." *Energy Economics* 18(1): 1–23.

Balk, B. 1998. *Industrial Price, Quantity, and Productivity Indices: The Microeconomic Theory and an Application*. Boston: Kluwer Academic Publishers.

———. 1999. "Scale Efficiency and Productivity Change." Paper presented at the Sixth European Productivity Workshop, October 29–31, Royal Agricultural University, Copenhagen.

Battese, G. E., and T. J. Coelli. 1992. "Frontier Production Functions, Technical Efficiency, and Panel Data: With Application to Paddy Farmers in India." In T. R. Gulledge and C. A. K. Lovell, eds., *International Applications of Productivity and Efficiency Analysis*. Boston: Kluwer Academic Publishers.

———. 1995. "A Model for Technical Inefficiency Effects in a Stochastic Frontier Production Function for Panel Data." *Empirical Economics* 20(2): 325–32.

Bauer, P. W. 1990. "Recent Developments in the Econometric Estimation of Frontiers." *Journal of Econometrics* 46(1–2): 39–56.

Bernstein, J. I., and D. E. M. Sappington. 1999. "Setting the X Factor in Price-Cap Regulation Plans." *Journal of Regulatory Economics* 16(1): 5–25.

Bhattacharyya, A., T. Harris, and N. Rangesan. 1995. "Allocative Efficiency of Rural Nevada Water Systems: A Hedonic Shadow Cost Function Approach." *Journal of Regional Science* 3: 485–501.

Bogetoft, P. 1994. "Incentive Efficiency Production Frontiers: An Agency Perspective on DEA." *Management Science* 40: 959–68.

———. 1995. "Incentives and Productivity Measurements." *International Journal of Production Economics* 39(1–2): 67–77.

———. 1997. "DEA-Based Yardstick Competition: The Optimality of Best Practice Regulation." *Annals of Operations Research* 73: 277–98.

Bravo-Ureta, B. E., and L. Rieger. 1991. "Dairy Farm Efficiency Measurement Using Stochastic Frontiers and Neoclassical Duality." *American Journal of Agricultural Economics* 73(2): 421–28.

Burns, P., M. Huggins, C. Riechmann, and T. Weyman-Jones. 2000. "Choice of Model and Availability of Data for the Efficiency Analysis of Dutch Network and Supply Businesses in the Electricity Sector." Dutch Electricity Regulatory Service, Office of Energy Regulation, The Hague. Processed.

Byrnes, P., S. Grosskoft, and K. Hayes. 1986. "Efficiency and Ownership: Further Evidence." *Review of Economics and Statistics* 68(2): 337–41.

Campos-Mendez, J., A. Estache, and L. Trujillo. 2001. "Processes, Information, and Accounting Gaps in the Regulation of Argentina's Private Railways." Policy Research Working Paper no. 2636. World Bank, Washington, D.C.

Carrington, R., T. J. Coelli, and E. Groom. 2002. "International Benchmarking for Monopoly Price Regulation: The Case of Australian Gas Distribution." *Journal of Regulatory Economics* 21(2): 191–216.

Caves, D. W., and L. R. Christensen. 1980. "The Relative Efficiency of Public and Private Firms in a Competitive Environment: The Case of Canadian Railroads." *Journal of Political Economy* 88(5): 958–76.

Caves, D. W., L. R. Christensen, and W. E. Diewert. 1982a. "Multilateral Comparisons of Output, Input, and Productivity Using Superlative Index Numbers." *Economic Journal* 92(365): 73–86.

———. 1982b. "The Economic Theory of Index Numbers and the Measurement of Input, Output, and Productivity." *Econometrica* 50(6): 1393–1414.

Caves, D. W., L. R. Christensen, and J. A. Swanson. 1981. "Productivity Growth, Scale Economies, and Capacity Utilization in U.S. Railroads, 1955–74." *American Economic Review* 71(5): 994–1002.

Coelli, T. J. 1996a. "A Guide to DEAP Version 2.1: A DEA (Computer) Program." Center for Efficiency and Productivity Analysis Working Paper no. 96/08. University of New England, Department of Econometrics, Armidale, Australia.

———. 1996b. "A Guide to FRONTIER Version 4.1: A Computer Program for Frontier Production Function Estimation." Center for Efficiency and Productivity Analysis Working Paper no. 96/07. University of New England, Department of Econometrics, Armidale, Australia.

———. 2000. "On the Econometric Estimation of the Distance Function Representation of a Production Technology." Catholic University of Louvain, Center for Operations Research and Econometrics, Louvain-la-Neuve, Belgium. Processed.

———. 2002. "A Comparison of Alternative Productivity Growth Measures: With Application to Electricity Generation." In K. Fox, ed., *Efficiency in the Public Sector.* Boston: Kluwer Academic Publishers.

Coelli, T. J., and R. A. Cuesta. 2000. "Simultaneous Equations Bias in Production Function Estimation: Revisiting an Old Debate." Catholic University of Louvain, Center for Operations Research and Econometrics, Louvain-la-Neuve, Belgium. Processed.

Coelli, T. J., and S. Perelman. 1999. "A Comparison of Parametric and Nonparametric Distance Functions: With Application to European Railways." *European Journal of Operations Research* 117(2): 326–39.

———. 2000. "Technical Efficiency of European Railways: A Distance Function Approach." *Applied Economics* 32(15): 1967–76.

Coelli, T. J., and D. S. P. Rao. 1999. "Implicit Value Shares in Malmquist TFP Index Numbers." Paper presented at the Sixth European Workshop on Efficiency and Productivity Analysis, October 29–31, Royal Agricultural University, Copenhagen.

Coelli, T. J., S. Perelman, and E. Romano. 1999. "Airlines, Environment, and Technical Efficiency: An International Comparative Study." *Journal of Productivity Analysis* 11(3): 251–73.

Coelli, T. J., D. S. P. Rao, and G. E. Battese. 1998. *An Introduction to Efficiency and Productivity Analysis* Boston: Kluwer Academic Publishers.

Coto, P., J. Baños, and A. Rodríguez. 2000. "Economic Efficiency in Spanish Ports: Some Empirical Evidence." *Maritime Policy and Management: International Journal of Shipping and Port Research* 27(2): 169–74.

Cowie, J., and G. Riddington. 1996. "Measuring the Efficiency of European Railways." *Applied Economics* 28(8): 1027–35.

Crain, W., and A. Zardkoohi. 1978. "A Test of the Property Rights Theory of the Firm: Water Utilities in the U.S." *Journal of Law and Economics* 21(2): 395–408.

Crampes, C., N. Diette, and A. Estache. 1990. "The Potential for Yardstick Competition in Brazil's Water Sector." World Bank, Washington, D.C. Processed.

Cullinane, K., and M. Khanna. 1998. "Economies of Scale in Large Container Ships.: *Journal of Transport* 32(2): 185–207.

Das, N. 2000 "Technology, Efficiency, and Sustainability of Competition in the Indian Telecommunications Sector." *Information Economics and Policy.* 12(2): 133–54.

de Boer, Boles. 1996. "The Economic Efficiency of Telecommunications in a Deregulated Market: The Case of New Zealand." *Economic Record* 72(16): 24–35.

Diewert, W. E. 2000. "Alternative Approaches to Measuring Productivity and Efficiency." Keynote paper presented at the North American Productivity Workshop, June 15–17, Union College, Schenectady, New York.

Dodgson, J. S. 1985. "A Survey of Recent Developments in the Measurement of Rail Total Factor Productivity." In K. J. Bulton and D. E. Pitfield, eds., *International Railway Economics.* London: Gower House.

————. 1994. "Railway Privatization." In M. Bishop, J. Kay, and C. Mayer, eds., *Privatization and Economic Performance.* New York: Oxford University Press.

Elteto, O., and P. Koves. 1964. "On a Problem of Index Number Computation Relating to International Comparison." *Statisztikai Szemle* 42: 507–18.

Estache, A., and E. Kouassi. 2002. "Sector Organization, Corruption, and the Inefficiency of African Water Utillities." World Bank, Washington, D.C. Processed.

Estache, A., and M. Rodriguez-Pardina. 2000. "Reforming the Electricity Sectors in the Southern Cone: The Chilean and Argentinean Experiments." In Luigi Manzetti, ed., *Regulatory Policy in Latin America: Post-Privatization Realities.* Miami: North-South Center Press, University of Miami.

Estache, A., and M. Rossi. 2002. " How Different Is the Efficiency of Public and Private Water Companies in Asia?" *World Bank Economic Review* 16(1): 139–48.

Estache, A., M. Gonzalez, and L. Trujillo. 2001. " Efficiency Gains from Port Reform and the Potential for Yardstick Competition: Lessons from Mexico." *World Development* 30(4): 545–60.

————. Forthcoming. "What Does Railways 'Privatization' Do for Efficiency? Evidence from Argentina and Brazil." *World Development.*

Estache, A., M. Rossi, and C. Ruzzier. 2002. "The Case for International Coordination of Eletricity Regulation: Evidence from the Measurement of Efficiency in South America." World Bank, Washington, D.C. Processed.

Färe, R., S. Grosskopf, C. A. K. Lovell, and C. Pasurka. 1989. "Multilateral Productivity Comparisons When Some Outputs Are Undesirable: A Nonparametric Approach." *Review of Economics and Statistics* 71(1): 90–98.

Färe, R., S. Grosskopf, M. Norris, and Z. Zhang. 1994. "Productivity Growth, Technical Progress, and Efficiency Changes in Industrialized Countries." *American Economic Review* 84(1): 66–83.

Farrell, M. J. 1957. "The Measurement of Productive Efficiency." *Journal of the Royal Statistical Society* A CXX(Part 3): 253–90.

Feigenbaum, S., and R. Teeples. 1984. "Public Versus Private Water Delivery: A Hedonic Cost Approach." *Review of Economics and Statistics* 65(4): 672–78.

Ferrier, G. D., and C. A. K. Lovell. 1990. "Measuring Cost Efficiency in Banking: Econometric and Linear Programming Evidence." *Journal of Econometrics* 46(1–2): 229–45.

Førsund, F. R., and S. A. C. Kittelsen. 1998. "Productivity Development of Norwegian Electricity Distribution Utilities." *Resource and Energy Economics* 20: 207–24.

Fox, W., and R. Hofler. 1986. "Using Homothetic Composed Error Frontiers to Measure Water Utility Efficiency." *Southern Economic Journal* 53(2): 461–77.

Fuss, M. 1994. "Productivity Growth in Canadian Telecommunications." *Canadian Journal of Economics* 27(2): 371–92.

Gathon, H. J., and S. Perelman. 1992. "Measuring Technical Efficiency in European Railways: A Panel Data Approach." *Journal of Productivity Analysis* 3(1–2): 131–51.

Giokas,D. I, and G. C. Pentzaropolulos. 2000. "Evaluating Productive Efficiency in Telecommunications: Evidence from Greece." *Telecommunications Policy* 24(8-9): 781–94.

Green, R., and M. Rodriguez-Pardina. 1999. *Resetting Price Controls for Privatized Utilities, A Manual for Regulators*. Development Studies. Washington, D.C.: World Bank Institute.

Grifell, E., and C. A. K. Lovell. 1999. "A Generalized Malmquist Productivity Index." *Sociedad de Estadística e Investigación Operativa* 7: 81–101.

Hjalmarsson, L., and A. Viederpass. 1992a. "Efficiency and Ownership in Swedish Electricity Distribution." *Journal of Productivity Analysis* 3(1–2): 7–24.

———. 1992b. "Productivity in Swedish Electricity Retail Distribution." *Scandinavian Journal of Economics* 94(0): 193–205.

Hunt, L., and E. Lynk. 1995. "Privatisation and Efficiency in the U.K. Water Industry: An Empirical Analysis." *Oxford Bulletin of Economics and Statistics* 57(3): 371–88.

Jamasb, T., and M. Pollitt. 2000. "Benchmarking and Regulation of Electricity Transmission and Distribution Utilities: Lessons from International Experience." University of Cambridge, Department of Applied Economics, Cambridge, U.K. Processed.

Kim, Y., and P. Schmidt. 2000. "A Review and Empirical Comparison of Bayesian and Classical Approaches to Inference on Efficiency Levels in Stochastic Frontier Models with Panel Data." *Journal of Productivity Analysis* 14(2).

Kim, T. Y., J. D. Lee, Y. H. Park, and B. Kim. 1999. "International Comparisons of Productivity and Its Determinants in the Natural Gas Industry." *Energy Economics* 21: 273–93.

Kumbhakar, S. C., and L. Hjalmarsson. 1998. "Relative Performance of Public and Private Ownership under Yardstick Competition: Electricity Retail Distribution." *European Economic Review* 42(1): 97–122.

Kumbhakar, S., and C. A. K. Lovell. 2000. *Stochastic Frontier Analysis*. Cambridge, U.K.: Cambridge University Press.

Laffont, J. J., and J. Tirole. 1993. *A Theory of Incentives in Procurement and Regulation.* Cambridge, Massachusetts: MIT Press.

Liu, Z. 1995. "The Comparative Performance of Public and Private Enterprises." *Journal of Transport Economics and Policy* 29(3): 263–74.

Martínez, E., R. Díaz, M. Navarro, and T. Ravelo. 1999. "A Study of the Efficiency of Spanish Port Authorities Using Data Envelopment Analysis." *International Journal of Transport Economics* 26(2): 237–53.

Morrison-Paul, C. 1999. *Cost Structure and the Measurement of Economic Performance.* Boston: Kluwer Academic Publishers.

Mundlak, Y. 1996. "Production Function Estimation: Reviving the Primal." *Econometrica* 64(2): 431–38.

Nash, C. 1985. "European Railways Comparisons—What Can We Learn?" In K. J. Bulton and D. E. Pitfield, eds., *International Railway Economics.* London: Gower House.

Newbery, D. M. 2000. *Privatization, Restructuring, and Regulation of Network Utilities.* Cambridge, Massachusetts: MIT Press.

Norsworthy, J., and D. Tsai. 1999. "Performance Measurement for Price Cap Regulation of Telecommunications. Using Evidence from a Cross-Section Study of United States Local Exchange Carriers." In M. Crew, ed., *Regulation under Increasing Competition.* Boston: Kluwer Academic Publisher.

Office of Energy Regulation. 2001. "Price Cap Regulation, Gas Distribution Companies 2002/2003." Consultation document 100350/1. The Hague.

Orea, L. 2002. "A Parametric Decomposition of a Generalized Malmquist Productivity Index." *Journal of Productivity Analysis* 18(1): 5–22.

Perelman, S., and P. Pestieau. 1988. "Technical Performance in Public Enterprises: A Comparative Study of Railways and Postal Services." *European Economic Review* 32(2–3): 432–41.

Pollitt, M. G. 1995. *Ownership and Performance in Electric Utilities.* Oxford, U.K.: Oxford University Press.

Roberts, M. J. 1986. "Economies of Density and Size in the Production and Delivery of Electric Power." *Land Economics* 62(4): 378–87.

Rodriguez-Alvarez, A. R. 2000. "Measuring Allocative Efficiency in a Bureaucracy: The Spanish Public Hospitals Sector." PhD Thesis, University of Oviedo, Oviedo, Spain.

Rodríguez-Pardina, M., and M. Rossi. 1999a. "Fronteras de eficiencia en el sector de distribución de energa electrica: la experiencia sudamericana." Discussion Paper no. 15. Center for Economic Studies on Regulation Issues. Universidad Argentina de la Empresa, Buenos Aires.

———. 1999b. "Medidas de eficiencia y regulación: una ilustracion del sector de distribuidoras de gas en la Argentina." Discussion Paper no. 14. Center for

Economic Studies on Regulation Issues. University Argentina de la Empresa, Buenos Aires.

Roll, Y., and Y. Hayuth. 1993. "Port Performance Comparison Applying Data Envelopment Analysis (DEA)." *Maritime Policy and Management: International Journal of Shipping and Port Research* 20(2): 153–61.

Rossi, M. 2001. "Technical Change and Efficiency Measures: The Post-Privatisation in the Gas Distribution Sector in Argentina." *Energy Economics* 23(3): 295–304.

Rossi, M., and C. Ruzzier. 2000. "On the Regulatory Application of Efficiency Measures." *Utilities Policy* 9(June): 81–92.

Rushdi, A. 1994. "Productivity Changes in the Gas and Fuel Corporation of Victoria." *Energy Economics* 16(1): 36–45.

———. 2000. "Total Factor Productivity Measures for Telstra." *Telecommunications Policy* 24(2): 143–54.

Ryan, D. L., and T. J. Wales. 2000. "Imposing Local Concavity in the Translog and Generalized Leontief Cost Functions." *Economic Letters* 67(3): 253–60.

Saal, D. S., and D. Parker. 2000. "Productivity and Price Performance in the Privatised Water and Sewerage Companies in England and Wales." Paper presented at the North American Productivity Workshop, June 15–17, Union College, Schenectady, New York.

Salvanes, K., and S. Tjotta. 1994. "Productivity Differences in Multiple Output Industries: An Empirical Application to Electricity Distribution." *Journal of Productivity Analysis* 5(1): 23–43.

Schmidt, P., and C. A. K. Lovell. 1979. "Estimating Technical and Allocative Inefficiency Relative to Stochastic Production and Cost Functions." *Journal of Econometrics* 9(3): 343–66.

Simar, L., and P. W. Wilson. 2000. "Statistical Inference in Nonparametric Frontier Models: The State of the Art." *Journal of Productivity Analysis* 13(1): 49–78.

Sueyoshi, T. 1994. "Stochastic Production Frontier Analysis: Measuring Performance of Public Telecommunications in 24 OECD Countries." *European Journal of Operational Research* 74: 466–78.

———. 1997. "Measuring Efficiency and Returns to Scale of Nippon Telegraph & Telephone in Production and Cost Analysis." *Management Science* 43: 779–96.

Szulc, B. J. 1964. "Indices for Multiregional Comparisons." *Prezeglad Statystyczny (Statistical Review)* 3: 239–54.

Tongzon, J. 2001. "Efficiency Measurement of Selected Australian and Other International Ports Using Data Envelopment Analysis." *Transportation Research Part A, Policy and Practice* 35(2): 113–28.

Waddams-Price, C., and T. Weyman-Jones. 1996. "Malmquist Indices of Productivity Change in the U.K. Gas Industry before and after Privatisation." *Applied Economics* 28(1): 29–39.

Weyman-Jones, T. G. 1991. "Productive Efficiency in a Regulated Industry: The Area Boards of England and Wales." *Energy Economics* 13(2):116–22.

———. 1992. "Problems of Yardstick Regulation in Electricity Distribution." In M. Bishop, J. Kay, C. Mayer, and D. Thompson, eds., *Privatisation and Regulation II.* Oxford, U.K.: Oxford University Press.

Weyman-Jones, T. G., and P. Burns. 1996. "Cost Functions and Cost Efficiency in Electricity Distribution: A Stochastic Frontier Approach." *Bulletin of Economic Research* 48(1): 41–64.

Zhang, Y., and R. Bartels. 1998. "The Effect of Sample Size on the Mean Efficiency in DEA: With an Application to Electricity Distribution in Australia, Sweden, and New Zealand." *Journal of Productivity Analysis* 9(3): 187–204.

Index